PRACTICAL GUIDE TO LITIGATION AND ARBITRATION
IN THE UNITED ARAB EMIRATES

ARAB AND ISLAMIC LAWS SERIES

Volume 26

Series General Editor
Dr. Mark S.W. Hoyle

The titles published in this series are listed at the end of this volume.

Practical Guide to Litigation and Arbitration in the United Arab Emirates

A detailed guide to litigation and arbitration in the United Arab Emirates based on Federal laws, laws specific to the individual Emirates, judgments delivered by the Court of Cassation and International Conventions to which the United Arab Emirates is a member.

First Edition

By
ESSAM AL TAMIMI
LLB (Al Ain) LLM (Harvard)
*Licenced Advocate of the Courts of the United Arab Emirates
Managing Partner of Al Tamimi & Co, United Arab Emirates*

KLUWER LAW INTERNATIONAL
THE HAGUE / LONDON / NEW YORK

Published by:
Kluwer Law International,
P.O. Box 85889, 2508 CN The Hague, The Netherlands
sales@kluwerlaw.com
http://www.kluwerlaw.com

Sold and distributed in North, Central and South America by:
Aspen Publishers, Inc.
7201 McKinney Circle, Frederick, MD 21704, USA

Sold and distributed in all other countries by:
Turpin Distribution Services Limited
Blackhorse Road, Letchworth, Herts.,
SG6 1HN, United Kingdom

A C.I.P Catalogue record for this book is available from the Library of Congress.

Printed on acid-free paper

ISBN 90-411-2221-4

All Rights Reserved
© 2003 Kluwer Law International

No part of this work may be reproduced, stored in a retrieval system, or transmitted in any form or by any means, electronic, mechanical, photocopying, microfilming, recording, or otherwise, without written permission from the Publisher, with the exception of any material supplied specifically for the purpose of being entered and executed on a computer system, for exclusive use by the purchaser of the work.

Printed and bound in Great Britain by Antony Rowe Limited

PREFACE

I am honoured to place the *Practical Guide to Litigation and Arbitration in the United Arab Emirates* before international and local legal practitioners as well as scholars. This book has truly been a summary of my practical experience of appearing and arguing cases before the Local and Federal Courts in the United Arab Emirates. I am privileged to be a first generation lawyer in the United Arab Emirates and to have had the tremendous experience of being part of the legal and judicial structure of the United Arab Emirates.

For me, the past 17 years of practice has been a journey of a lifetime. The UAE has progressed from having a few laws and regulations, Courts mixed between Islamic Shari'a and Civil Courts to the introduction of modern laws which have rapidly developed the UAE into a modern civil and commercial legal system. It has been a wonderful experience watching the growth and being a part of it.

The aim of this book is to provide useful and practical guidance on all aspects of litigation and arbitration in the United Arab Emirates. The focus of this work is the Federal Law No. 11 of 1992 on Civil Procedures (which I refer to throughout as the "Civil Procedure Law"). I have also referred to certain local laws and decrees which are relevant. While I have attempted to refer to specific articles in the Civil Procedure Law, the real value of this work may lie where there is no specific article in point, where a practice has arisen or developed over the years in the courts. I have also referred to cases from the Federal Supreme Court of Cassation (which I refer to as the "Supreme Court of Cassation") and from the Dubai Court of Cassation which have been carefully selected and introduced as guidelines and references for different sections of this specialized book dealing with litigation and arbitration in the United Arab Emirates.

In writing this book I have had the pleasure of working and discussing the contents with my colleagues at Al Tamimi & Company. I also wish to acknowledge the work and the extensive effort made by Janet Bellamy without whose help it would not have been possible. She has contributed to the content, style and the language of the book, for which I am grateful. I am also grateful to Fatma El Zeini for the invaluable assistance and the research carried out by her and to Lucy Tholath in developing this book.

This book is the first of its kind on this subject and I hope that it will assist international and local jurists and legal practitioners to understand litigation and dispute resolution in the United Arab Emirates and how it is currently being conducted.

Essam Al Tamimi
United Arab Emirates
2003

CONTENTS

	Page
Preface...	v
Table of Statutes...	xiii

Chapter One

THE LEGAL SYSTEM IN THE UNITED ARAB EMIRATES................	1
1.1 Constitutional Overview...	1
1.2 The Federal Government..	2
1.2.1 *The Supreme Council*.......................................	2
1.2.2 *The Cabinet of Ministers*................................	3
1.2.3 *The National Assembly*...................................	3
1.2.4 *The Judicial Arrangements*.............................	4
1.3 The Legal System...	5
1.3.1 *A Civil Law System*..	5
1.3.2 *Legal Education*..	6
1.3.3 *Professional Associations*..............................	7

Chapter Two

THE COURTS...	9
2.1 The Judiciary...	9
2.1.1 *Notary Public*..	9
2.2 General Structure of the Courts............................	10
2.2.1 *Civil Courts*..	11
2.2.2 *Criminal Courts*..	12
2.2.3 *The Shari'a Courts*.......................................	14
2.2.4 *The Court of Cassation*.................................	15
2.2.5 *Special Tribunals*...	17
2.3 Court Fees...	17

Chapter Three

JURISDICTION AND FORUM..	19
3.1 International Jurisdiction.....................................	19
3.2 Domestic Jurisdiction...	21
3.3 Jurisdiction Over Property....................................	23
3.3.1 *Real Estate and Granted Land*.........................	23

	3.3.2	Movable Property	23
3.4		Jurisdiction in Respect of Subject Matter	25
	3.4.1	Labour Jurisdiction	25
	3.4.2	Rent Disputes	25
	3.4.3	Administrative Jurisdiction	26
	3.4.4	Jurisdiction over Free Zones	27
3.5		Choice of Forum	29
3.6		Choice of Law	29
3.7		Enforcement of Foreign Judgments	31
3.8		Treaties	33
	3.8.1	Gulf Co-Operation Council Convention	33
	3.8.2	Bilateral Treaty for the Enforcement of Judgments with France	36
	3.8.3	Reciprocal Agreement between the UAE and India	38

Chapter Four

COMMENCEMENT OF PROCEEDINGS			41
4.1		Initiating Action	41
	4.1.1	Reconciliation Committees at the Federal Courts	41
	4.1.2	Statement of Claim	43
	4.1.3	The Summons	45
4.2		Service	45
	4.2.1	Local Service	46
	4.2.2	Service in Another Emirate	47
	4.2.3	Service of Summons in a Foreign Jurisdiction	48
	4.2.4	Alternative Methods of Service	48
	4.2.5	Service to be Effected Twice	50
	4.2.6	Challenging the Service of Summons	52
4.3		Proceeding with the Main Action	52
	4.3.1	The Defendant's Response	52
	4.3.2	Preliminary Defences	53
4.4		Counterclaim	54
4.5		Interlocutory Applications	56
4.6		Witnesses	56
4.7		Expert Witnesses	58
	4.7.1	Duties of the Expert	59
4.8		Documents	60
4.9		Discovery	62
4.10		Joinder	63
4.11		Actions filed by or against Minors	65

Chapter Five

JUDGMENTS..		67
5.1	Judgment...	67
5.2	Default Judgment...	68
5.3	Judgment in the Presence of Both Parties..................	69
5.4	The Claimant's Failure to Attend Court....................	69
5.5	Interim Judgments..	70
5.6	Summary Judgment..	71

Chapter Six

ATTACHMENTS AND URGENT APPLICATIONS...........................			73
6.1	Attachments...		73
	6.1.1	*Procedure..*	75
	6.1.2	*Application for an Attachment Prior to the Main Action...*	76
	6.1.3	*Application for an Attachment after a Main Action is Filed...*	78
6.2	Objection to an Attachment Order.........................		80
	6.2.1	*Objection by the Claimant.............................*	81
	6.2.2	*The Defendant's Objection.............................*	82
6.3	Appeal...		83
6.4	Enforcement of Attachment Orders........................		85
	6.4.1	*Attachment Minutes....................................*	86
	6.4.2	*The Custodian...*	87
	6.4.3	*Problems in Attachment...............................*	88
	6.4.4	*Third Party Challenge.................................*	89
6.5	Sale of Attached Assets.....................................		90
6.6	Attachment of Land..		90
6.7	Disposing of the Assets Before the Order is Enforced		91
6.8	Urgent Applications..		92
	6.8.1	*Application to Survey or Document Status..............*	92
	6.8.2	*Application for a Witness to be heard Prior to the Main Action...*	93
	6.8.3	*Deputation from Another Court to hear a Witness or to order a Party to Produce Documents................*	94
	6.8.4	*Application to Appoint a Custodian....................*	94

Chapter Seven

EXECUTION PROCEEDINGS.. 97
    7.1   Execution... 97
    7.2   Procedure.. 98
        7.2.1   *Notice*.. 99
        7.2.2   *Application*... 99
    7.3   Challenging the Execution Proceedings................ 100
    7.4   Sale by Auction... 102
        7.4.1   *Auctioning Movable Property*....................... 104
        7.4.2   *Auctioning Immovable Property*................... 109
    7.5   Distribution of Sale Proceeds.............................. 114
        7.5.1   *Order of Distribution*................................... 115
    7.6   Destruction of goods by the Execution Court......... 118
    7.7   Conclusion of the Execution Procedure................. 119
    7.8   Imprisonment for Failure to Pay.......................... 120
    7.9   Execution in Criminal Matters............................ 122

Chapter Eight

APPEAL.. 125
    8.1   Preliminary Procedure.. 125
        8.1.1   *Notice of Appeal*... 126
    8.2   Appeal Proceedings.. 128
    8.3   Matters not subject to Appeal.............................. 128
        8.3.1   *Court of Appeal*.. 128
        8.3.2   *Court of Cassation*...................................... 129
    8.4   Appeal prior to Final Judgment........................... 129
    8.5   Appeal after Final Judgment............................... 130
        8.5.1   *Counter-Appeal and Sub-Appeal*................... 131
        8.5.2   *Decisions of the Court of Appeal*.................. 133
    8.6   Appeal to the Court of Cassation......................... 134
        8.6.1   *Notice*.. 137
        8.6.2   *Application to Suspend the Execution of Judgment*.... 138
        8.6.3   *Judgment of the Court of Cassation*.............. 140
    8.7   Review of Judgments.. 143

Chapter Nine

ARBITRATION.. 147
    9.1   Introduction... 147
    9.2   Formalities.. 149

9.3	Jurisdiction		149
9.4	Urgent and Interlocutory Applications		150
9.5	The Arbitration Tribunal		151
	9.5.1	*Duties of an Arbitrator*	152
	9.5.2	*Powers of the Arbitrators*	153
9.6	The Arbitration Award		154
9.7	Arbitration under the Supervision of the Court		155
9.8	Enforcement of the Award		156
9.9	Enforcement of a Foreign Arbitration Award		157
9.10	Appeal		160
9.11	Costs		161

Appendix 1: Table of Court Fees 163

Appendix 2: Table of Treaties, Conventions and International
Agreements 167

General Index 173

TABLE OF STATUTES

Arbitration Regulation No. 1 for the year 2001, pursuant to the Stocks and Commodities Law No. 4 of 2000.

Civil Transactions Law, (the "Civil Code"), Federal Law No. 5 of 1985.

Civil Procedure Law, (the "Civil Procedure Law"), Federal Law No. 11 of 1992.

Commercial Transactions Law, (the "Commercial Code"), Federal Law No. 18 of 1993.

Constitution, the Provisional Constitution of the UAE, dated 18 July 1971 made final by Constitutional Amendment No. 1 of 1996 (the "Constitution"), dated 2 December 1996.

Court Fees, Dubai Law No. 1 of 1994.

Criminal Law, (the "Penal Code), Federal Law No. 3 of 1987.

Criminal Procedure Law, Federal Law No. 35 of 1992.

Dubai Courts, Dubai Law No. 3 of 1992, Law forming the Courts in Dubai.

Dubai Law No. 4 of 1997, concerning Litigation against the Government of Dubai.

Dubai Law No. 6 of 1997, concerning Contracts of Government Departments in the Emirate of Dubai.

Dubai Law No. 5 of 2001, concerning the Use of Computers in Criminal Procedures.

Dubai Rent Committee: Decree No. 2 of 1993 regarding formation of a special Judicial Committee for Reconciliation of Disputes between Tenants and Landlords.

Electronic Commerce, Dubai Law No. 2 of 2002 concerning Electronic Transactions and Commerce.

Emirates, (Regulating the Judicial Relationship between the Emirates), Federal Law No. 11 of 1973.

Evidence, the Law of Proof in Civil and Commercial Transactions, Federal Law No. 10 of 1992.

Federal Courts, Federal Law No. 6 for the year 1978 concerning the Establishment of the Federal Courts, as amended by Federal Laws No. 2 of 1990, No. 5 of 1986 and No. 18 of 1991. Federal Law No. 10 of 1978 regarding the Federal Supreme Court as amended.

Federal Judicial Authority, the law of Judicial Authority, Federal Law No. 3 of 1983, as amended.

Labour Law, Federal Law No. 8 of 1980, (as amended by Federal Laws No. 24 of 1981, No. 15 of 1985 and No. 12 of 1986).

Landlord and Tenant in Sharjah: Law No. 6 of 2001.

Legal Profession, Federal Law No. 23 of 1991.

Maritime Code, Federal Law No. 26 of 1981, as amended by Federal Law No. 11 of 1988.

Perpetual Treaty of Maritime Truce 1850's.

Public Notary Law, Federal Law No. 22 of 1991.

Ras Al Khaimah Law of 1971, Law for establishing the Ras Al Khaimah Courts.

Reconciliation Committees: Federal Law No. 4 of 2001, (amending Federal Law No. 26 for 1999) regarding establishment of Reconciliation Committees at Federal Courts in the UAE.

Stocks and Commodities Law No. 4 for the year 2000.

Chapter One

THE LEGAL SYSTEM IN THE UNITED ARAB EMIRATES

1.1 Constitutional Overview

The United Arab Emirates is a federation of seven Emirates founded on 2nd December 1971 by the passing of the Union Declaration which declared the UAE an independent country. Prior to that, the Emirates fell under the protection of Britain in accordance with treaty agreements dating back to the Perpetual Treaty of Maritime Truce signed in the 1850's. It was this agreement which gave the UAE its former name of the Trucial States.

The UAE is governed in accordance with the Constitution of the United Arab Emirates. The Provisional Constitution was signed on the 18th of July 1971. Abu Dhabi, Dubai, Sharjah, Ajman, Um Al Quwain and Fujairah were the initial signatories and Ras Al Khaimah joined the Federation on the 10th of February 1972. The Provisional Constitution, with some minor amendments, was made final in terms of Constitutional Amendment Law No. 1 of 1996 (the "Constitution") and signed by the President of the UAE on the 2nd of September 1996. Islam is the official religion and Arabic is the official language of the UAE.

The Constitution provides that each Emirate may have a legislative body as well as a cabinet of ministers independent from that of the Federal Government. Although none of the Emirates in the UAE has a cabinet of ministers, Abu Dhabi, Dubai and Sharjah have an Executive Council. Each individual Emirate administers its local affairs through local government departments headed by a director general or a chairman. The supreme authority in each Emirate is the Ruler who is empowered to carry out the executive authority as well as the legislative authority within that Emirate. Laws are normally enacted in an Emirate by decree from the Ruler.

The Federal Government has exclusive jurisdiction over matters such as foreign affairs, defence, health and education.[1] The individual Emirates have exclusive jurisdiction over other matters of more regional concern unless they have otherwise surrendered such powers to the Federal Government.[2]

All the Emirates of the UAE contribute to the UAE Federal Budget though each Emirate has its own budget. Normally, the Federal Government operates and contributes towards the general services and utilities of the UAE as a whole whereas the local government in each individual Emirate is responsible for that Emirate. The Constitution provides that the natural resources and wealth of each Emirate shall be the property of that Emirate.[3]

1.2 The Federal Government

The Federal Government is headed by the President and consists of the Supreme Council, the Prime Minister and Cabinet of Ministers and the National Assembly.

1.2.1 The Supreme Council

The Supreme Council is the highest governmental authority in the UAE and it consists of the Rulers of each of the seven Emirates. While the Supreme Council is empowered to elect the President from the members of the Supreme Council every five Gregorian years, His Highness Sheikh Zayed Bin Sultan Al Nahyan has been the President of the UAE and the Ruler of Abu Dhabi since the formation of the UAE. The Supreme Council approves and signs all Federal laws before they are enacted and decides the government's policy on the UAE's political affairs. Decisions on substantive matters are taken by a majority of five, provided that this majority includes the votes of the Emirates of Abu Dhabi and Dubai.[4] Decisions on procedural matters are taken by simple majority.

---

[1] Articles 120 and 121 of the Constitution.

[2] Article 122 of the Constitution.

[3] Article 23 of the Constitution.

[4] Article 49 of the Constitution.

1.2.2   The Cabinet of Ministers

The Federal Government is administered by the Cabinet of Ministers which consists of the Prime Minister and his Ministers. The Cabinet is based in the capital of the UAE in the Emirate of Abu Dhabi. The Cabinet of Ministers are usually selected and nominated by the Prime Minister and then approved by the President following the concession of the Supreme Council. The Ministers themselves are citizens of the UAE drawn from the different Emirates,[1] the Prime Minister is however, usually elected from the ruling family of the Emirate of Dubai. At present, the Prime Minister of the UAE is His Highness Sheikh Maktoum Bin Rashid Al Maktoum, the Ruler of Dubai and member of the Supreme Council. There is no fixed term of office for the Cabinet of Ministers.

1.2.3   The National Assembly

The National Assembly consists of citizens of the United Arab Emirates and its members are drawn from reputable and respected members of the community of each individual Emirate. The members of the National Assembly are not elected to office but are recommended by the Ruler of each individual Emirate. The term of office for the members of the National Council is two years and is renewable upon the recommendation of the Ruler of the Emirate concerned. Those who serve on the National Assembly usually represent the interests of each Emirate as well as the interests of the UAE Federal Government before the National Assembly.[2] There are 40 members of the National Assembly and the number of representatives for each Emirate is based on the size of the Emirate. The allocation is presently as follows:

Abu Dhabi	-------8
Dubai	-------8
Sharjah	-------6
Ras Al Khaimah	-------6
Ajman	-------4
Fujairah	-------4
Umm Al Quwain	-------4

The decisions of the National assembly are advisory and neither the Cabinet nor the Supreme Council are obliged to follow them.

---

[1] Article 56 of the Constitution.

[2] Article 77 of the Constitution.

1.2.4   The Judicial Arrangements

The UAE Constitution permits each Emirate to have the power to retain its own judicial system, and accordingly there are Federal courts and "local" courts in the UAE.

The Emirates of Abu Dhabi, Sharjah, Ajman, Fujairah and Umm Al Quwain have transferred their judicial systems to the UAE Federal Judicial Authority. The judicial systems of these Emirates are therefore administered and supervised by the Ministry of Justice of the Federal Government. The Emirates of Dubai and Ras Al Khaimah have retained their own judicial systems which are not part of the UAE Federal Judicial Authority. As such there are no Federal courts within the Emirates of Dubai and Ras Al Khaimah and all matters within these Emirates are determined by the "local" courts. Judgments delivered by the Federal Courts of Appeal (Abu Dhabi, Sharjah, Fujairah, Ajman and Umm al Quwain) are subject to an appeal to the Federal Supreme Court of Cassation based in Abu Dhabi. Judgments delivered by the Dubai Court of Appeal are subject to an appeal to the Dubai Court of Cassation, there is no Court of Cassation in Ras Al Khaimah.

Each Emirate has its own jurisdiction, independent of Federal jurisdiction.[1] An agreement has also been signed by all the Emirates to facilitate co-operation between the judiciaries of each Emirate.

The local courts and the Federal courts apply the UAE Federal law enacted by the Supreme Council as well as the local law and regulations enacted by the Ruler of the Emirate concerned. Although the legal procedures and law applicable in individual Emirates are similar there are some differences. In the event of a conflict between the Federal law and the local law, the Federal law will supersede the local law.[2]

The police force and the prosecutor's office in the United Arab Emirates are Federal except in the Emirate of Dubai. Dubai has its own police force as well as its own prosecutor's office which are independent from the Federal government. The police force and the prosecutor's office apply the UAE Federal law apart from certain differences arising from the application of local law of the Emirate of Dubai.

---

[1] Dubai Court of Cassation Judgment 176/96 dated 8 March 1997, Dubai Court of Cassation Judgment 3/2000 dated 29 April 2000.

[2] Dubai Court of Cassation Judgment 324/2001 dated 25 November 2001.

1.3 The Legal System

1.3.1 A Civil Law System

The UAE legal system is based on the civil law system and as such the primary source of law is a statutory code. The UAE legal system has been influenced to a large extent by the Egyptian legal system which has its source in French and Roman law. The law in the UAE has also naturally been influenced by Islamic Law codified in the Shari'a and embodied in the UAE civil and commercial law.

The civil law system not only applies to the codification of laws in the UAE but also to the practice and procedure of the judicial system. Judges, for instance do not normally hear oral argument and precedents are not judicially binding, although they are used as persuasive argument before the courts.[1]

In addition, because of the nature of Dubai in particular as a commercial center and because of the presence of international law firms with "common law" roots, many contracts which have been drafted in the UAE appear to have been influenced by common law principles.

This has created difficulties in the application of the law to these contracts by the courts of the UAE since the judicial authority does not recognise some of the principles or the practices of the common law system. For example:

1. As is usual in a civil law system, the Judge is under no obligation to take into consideration previous decisions of the court as precedents in an action before him.[2]
2. In a construction contract a party legitimately seeking to rely on the *force majeure* clause of a contract may be prevented by the Judge from doing so because of the provisions on the UAE law of tort.[3]
3. There is no system of discovery of documents.
4. Mareva injunctions and Anton Pillar orders are not available.

---

[1] Dubai Court of Cassation Judgment 407/94 dated 25 June 1995.

[2] Supreme Court of Cassation Judgment 120 for the year 18 dated 25 June 1996. Supreme Court of Cassation Judgment 300 for the year 18 dated 30 September 1997. Dubai Court of Cassation Judgment 407/94 dated 25 June 1995.

[3] Supreme Court of Cassation Judgment 353 for the year 20 dated 26 April 1998.

1.3.2 Legal Education

Legal education is relatively new to the UAE. The UAE University in Al Ain is the only university in the UAE providing a degree course in law and was only established in 1978, another law school is however planned in Sharjah. Most UAE nationals who have studied law received their legal education at a university in Egypt or in recent years from the UAE University in Al Ain with a few obtaining law degrees from universities in the United Kingdom and America.

Very few Judges in the UAE are UAE nationals. Normally, Judges who sit in the UAE courts are citizens of other Arab countries who have been seconded to the UAE under special agreements with their respective governments or by direct employment with the Ministry of Justice or the court in the case of Dubai. Almost 90 per cent of Judges in the UAE courts are from Egypt, Syria, Lebanon, Sudan and a few from North African countries.

In the United Arab Emirates a person may obtain admission to a UAE law school provided he has the required minimum average in his high school results. The training at the UAE University Law School is conducted in Arabic and the lecturers and professors are citizens of the UAE or other Arab countries (who have been seconded to teach at the UAE University).

Law graduates in the UAE who do not choose to go into private practice often choose to become prosecutors and serve as a public prosecutor for the Ministry of Justice, or the Dubai or Ras Al Khaimah Judicial Authorities. A few of these prosecutors may be promoted to become Judges to serve at the courts.

Law graduates seeking to be admitted to practice as a lawyer in the UAE must apply to the Ministry of Justice to be licensed as a lawyer in the UAE. To obtain a license to practice as a lawyer the applicant must hold at least a four-year law degree from an approved university law school. Legal courses attended over a one or two-year period will not be acknowledged in the UAE as a law degree. Appearance by advocates before all courts is restricted by law to UAE nationals with a valid licence. An exception is made to some practicing Arab lawyers already licenced before the law restricting appearance before the courts by nationals was passed.

Following the preliminary approval of their application, a law graduate will then be assigned to a law firm to work as a trainee lawyer for a period of twelve months. The Ministry of Justice will pay the trainee lawyer a monthly remuneration of AED 5,000 (approximately USD 1,370). Law firms are not required to pay trainee lawyers, however, some do so at their discretion. During the twelve-month training period, a trainee lawyer will appear before the court accompanied by a licensed lawyer from the firm in which they are being trained. Every month a report on the conduct and the training of the trainee lawyer is prepared by the law firm and forwarded to the Ministry of Justice. Following the completion of the training a report will be filed with the Ministry of Justice setting out the trainee lawyers' court attendances and work experience. The Ministry of Justice will provide final approval of their application and will issue a licence to the trainee lawyer to practice as a lawyer within the UAE after they have sworn the required oath and been entered into the register of lawyers maintained by the Ministry of Justice. There are no professional admission examination requirements for admission as a lawyer in the UAE following the one-year training course. The Ministry of Justice will then renew the licence on an annual basis.

Lawyers who wish to practice in the Emirate of Dubai and/or the Emirate of Ras Al Khaimah must also obtain a further local licence. Lawyers who are licensed by the Federal Ministry of Justice will not have an automatic right to practice before the courts in the Emirates of Dubai and Ras Al Khaimah unless they have an independent licence from these two Emirates. The register of lawyers in these Emirates is usually maintained by the Director of the courts in co-operation with the Ruler's office of the relevant Emirate.

1.3.3   Professional Associations

The UAE has no Bar Association for lawyers, as the UAE makes no distinction between solicitors and barristers. The Ministry of Justice supervises the training, licensing and the conduct of all lawyers within the UAE though a committee comprised of a representative from each of the Ministry of Justice and the Public Prosecutor's office and a senior practicing member of the legal profession within the UAE.

The UAE does however have a Jurist Association consisting of lawyers, Judges, legal advisers and consultants. The Jurist Association has offices in Sharjah and Abu Dhabi and is administered by an elected committee comprised of its members and chairman. The Jurist Association in the UAE is not an official body and does not have any official supervisory powers over lawyers. Its objectives are as follows:

1. To have an in-depth knowledge of and to promote research in the Islamic Shari'a as the major source of law in the UAE.
2. To recognise and defend human rights and justice.
3. To enhance the standard of legal practitioners professionally and intellectually.
4. To encourage ties and co-operation between the association and other organisations in the UAE.
5. To establish co-operation and contact with government departments and public entities.
6. To co-operate with other juristic associations and bar associations in the Arab world and internationally.
7. To comment and provide opinion on the new legislation enacted in the UAE.
8. To encourage legal research to hold seminars and conferences.
9. To participate in the development of the advocacy practice in the UAE including the training of lawyers in co-operation with the relevant departments in charge.
10. To protect the lawyers' profession and legal practitioners in the UAE according to the laws and regulations.

The formation of a Bar Association, restricted to nationals, had been proposed by a number of lawyers and in May 2001 it was agreed to form a Bar Association independent of the Jurist Association. A Board was elected, a Constitution approved and the association now awaits Federal and Local approval.

Chapter Two

THE COURTS

The UAE courts adjudicate civil matters in accordance with the Federal Law No. 11 of 1992 issuing the Law of Civil Procedure, which will be referred to as the "Civil Procedure Law" in this text. The courts adjudicate criminal matters in accordance with the Federal Law No. 35 of 1992 issuing the law of Criminal Procedure and other laws dealing with specific crimes such as those dealt with in telecommunication, trademark and copyright laws.

These laws set out in detail the law and procedure for conducting civil and criminal cases before the UAE courts, whether Federal or local.

2.1 The Judiciary

Judges of the Federal Courts of the UAE are recommended by the Ministry of Justice and appointed by a decree of the Supreme Council. All Judges are independent from the Ministry of Justice and are subject only to the law. Local Judges such as those in Dubai are similarly recommended, however they are appointed by the Ruler's decree. Judges may not be removed or their employment terminated, except if they have resigned, or it is proved that they are incompetent, or where their secondment has come to an end.[1]

2.1.1 Notary Public

Certain documents which are to be presented in court or as required by law, are required to be notarised by a notary public. There is no provision for private notaries or lawyers to authenticate documents in the UAE. Only "Court Notaries" who are licensed and recognised by law are authorised to authenticate documents.[2]

---

[1] The Law of Judicial Authority, Federal Law No. 3 of 1983 as amended.
[2] Public Notary Law, Federal Law No. 22 of 1991.

Each court in the UAE has a notary public who sits at the court premises in each Emirate. The Court Notary may assign another notary to sit at the Chamber of Commerce or at the Department of Economic Development such as those of Dubai and Abu Dhabi.

The Court Notary will not only authenticate the signature of the party, but also on some occasions will ensure that the document complies with UAE law. The Court Notary will refuse to notarise documents which are contrary to UAE public policy or contrary to the law. He will request evidence that a person who is signing on behalf of a company has authority to do so and such authority will be recorded. The Court Notary will retain a copy of the relevant documents together with evidence of the identity of the party concerned in his register for his records.

A document will only be considered notarised once the relevant fees have been paid and once it has been signed and stamped by the Court Notary. Notarising documents will not add much to the evidence.[1] The only aspect that the notarisation of the documents will achieve is to confirm the identity of the party who has signed the document and the date on which the document was notarised. However, on some occasions as required by the law, certain documents will only be admissible upon notarisation. Ordinary agreements, however, need not be notarised unless otherwise stipulated by law.

2.2 General Structure of the Courts

As mentioned, the courts in the UAE are constitutionally divided into the Federal court[2] which is supervised by the Federal Ministry of Justice; and the local court which currently only exists in the Emirates of Dubai[3] and Ras Al Khaimah[4] and which are supervised by the Judicial Authority in those Emirates.

Both branches are, however governed to a large extent by the same law and procedure. There are minor differences in procedure, for instance, the court fees in the Emirates of Dubai and Ras Al Khaimah differ. The substantive law may also differ because the local courts will apply local laws in

---

[1] Supreme Court of Cassation Judgment 188 for the year 19 dated 11 May 1999.

[2] Federal Law No. 6 of 1978 concerning the establishment of the Federal courts as amended by Federal Law No. 2 of 1990.

[3] Dubai Law No. 3 of 1992, Law forming the Courts in the Emirate of Dubai.

[4] Ras Al Khaimah Law of 1971, Law for establishing the Ras Al Khaimah Courts.

addition to Federal laws to the extent to which they are not in conflict with the Federal laws. In the event of a conflict, the Federal laws will prevail.

Both the Federal and local courts are divided into three main courts, the civil courts, the criminal courts and the Shari'a court (Islamic court).

2.2.1 Civil Courts

The civil courts in the UAE deal with civil matters of any nature including private suits, debt recovery, banking, maritime, bankruptcy, intellectual property, company and insurance matters. Any action with a claim amounting to AED 100,000 or more will be heard before a bench of three Judges. A claim amounting to less than AED 100,000 will be heard by one Judge. Where the court consists of three Judges, judgment may be delivered by majority or unanimously.

Most of the arguments presented to the court are by way of written submissions or "memoranda" and it is usual for a case to be adjourned several times while the parties exchange pleadings and documentation before the matter is reserved for judgment. The civil courts may, upon the request of either party, call witnesses or refer the matter to an expert for an expert opinion on a factual or technical matter.

Any judgment delivered by a civil court is subject to the right of appeal to the Court of Appeal within 30 days calculated from the date following the day of judgment. The civil Court of Appeal consists of three Judges and judgments of the civil Court of Appeal may be delivered by majority or unanimously. The grounds of appeal can be based on either factual or legal matters and either party may submit further evidence or submit a request to hear witnesses to the civil Court of Appeal. While arguments may be made orally, arguments are usually made to the Court of Appeal by written submissions.

Federal judgments delivered by the Federal Courts of Appeal (Abu Dhabi, Sharjah, Fujairah, Ajman and Umm al Quwain) are subject to an appeal to the Supreme Court of Cassation based in Abu Dhabi. Judgments delivered by the Dubai Court of Appeal are subject to an appeal to the Dubai Court of Cassation, there is no Court of Cassation in Ras Al Khaimah. This right of appeal is automatic if the claim amounts to more than AED 10,000,[1] if not, the leave of the court is required. The grounds of appeal to the Supreme Court of Cassation and the Dubai Court of Cassation may only be based

---

[1] Dubai Court of Cassation Judgment no 25/97 dated 11 October 1997.

upon matters of law.[1] Generally, the submission of further documents or evidence into court is not permitted, however, in very exceptional circumstances the Court of Cassation may grant the parties leave to submit specific documents.[2]

2.2.2 Criminal Courts

Criminal actions in the UAE commence with the filing of a complaint with the local police in the jurisdiction where the offence was committed. During the investigation, the police may take the statement of any parties involved. The matter is thereafter usually referred by the local police to the prosecutor's office within 48 hours. The police may refer the matter to the Prosecutor for advice prior to registering the claim.

The prosecutor's office will then investigate the matter, take the statements of any parties involved, and hear their witnesses or any other person that the Prosecutor may consider to be appropriate. The prosecutor's office will then decide whether to refer the matter to the court or to close the matter on the basis that there is no crime. The role of the prosecutor's office is to investigate and prosecute criminal matters in the UAE and the prosecutor's office will not attend to any civil matters. The jurisdiction, powers and procedures of the prosecutor's office are set out in the Federal Law of Criminal Procedure No. 35 of 1992.

If the prosecutor's office is of the view that a crime is sufficiently substantiated by the evidence gathered then the matter will be referred to the courts. A hearing date will be scheduled and the accused will be asked to come before the Judge to answer for the crime of which he or she is accused. There are three types of crimes namely felonies, misdemeanours and contraventions.[3] Normally a misdemeanour involves a less serious crime which carries a sentence of a fine or imprisonment of up to three years. A felony is more serious and includes any crime which is punishable by a sentence of more than three years, to life imprisonment or execution. A misdemeanour will be heard by one Judge whereas a felony will be heard by a panel of three Judges.[4]

---

[1] Supreme Court of Cassation Judgment 512 for the year 19 dated 28 September 1999, Dubai Court of Cassation Judgment 188/93 dated 29 January 1994, Dubai Court of Cassation Judgment 238/95 dated 6 July 1996.

[2] Supreme Court of Cassation Judgment 231 for the year 10 dated 18 April 1989.

[3] Article 26 of the Penal Code, Federal Law No. 3 of 1987.

[4] Article 139 of the Criminal Law of Procedure.

Criminal courts in the UAE apply the UAE Penal Code, Federal Law No. 3 of 1987 and the UAE Criminal Law of Procedure, Federal Law No. 35 of 1992 together with sections contained in other laws which provide for specific crimes.

Usually, the accused will be asked by the court to plead at the first hearing, either personally or be accompanied by his attorney. The court will appoint an attorney if the person cannot afford one for crimes which are punishable by a sentence of life imprisonment or execution.

Litigation in criminal matters is usually based on questioning and cross-examination of witnesses whose statements were taken by the police or the prosecutor's office as well as of the accused. Written submissions and evidence are also allowed by the court. The parties may call experts and the court may appoint its own experts upon the request of either party or at the Judge's discretion.

The plaintiff in all criminal matters is the State represented by the prosecutor's office. The victim will not stand as a plaintiff in a criminal matter even if he or she has initiated the complaint with the police as he or she has no *locus standi* before the criminal courts. A victim may, however, file a separate civil action seeking damages or a civil remedy which may be joined with the criminal action. In such a case the criminal Judge will hear the civil matter as well as the criminal matter though the emphasis will be on the criminal case. The leave of the court is required to join a civil action with a criminal action and it is entirely at the Judge's discretion. If the leave of the court is given for the civil action to be joined with the criminal action then the prosecutor will argue the criminal case and the victim will argue the civil claim.

Any sentence ordered by the court will be enforced immediately in spite of the fact that the accused has the automatic right to appeal within 15 days of the judgment. If an appeal is filed, it is at the discretion of the Court of Appeal to suspend the sentence and the court may release the accused on bail pending the outcome of the appeal. The matter will be considered by three Judges at the Court of Appeal. The prosecutor's office also has an automatic right to appeal within 15 days of the judgment and the Attorney General within 30 days of the judgment. Again, the appeal will be before three Judges at the Court of Appeal. The Court of Appeal will review both matters of fact and law. The Court of Appeal may also admit further documentary evidence and hear witnesses of both parties before delivering its judgment on the matter.

Any judgment delivered by the Criminal Court of Appeal will be subject to an appeal to the Supreme Court of Cassation in Abu Dhabi for the Federal court and in Dubai to the Dubai Court of Cassation. Appeal to the Supreme Court of Cassation in Abu Dhabi or the Court of Cassation in Dubai must be filed within 30 days from the date of the judgment and may be based only on matters of law. No further evidence or witnesses or review of factual matters will be permitted. Any sentence ordered or confirmed by the Court of Appeal will be enforced immediately even if an appeal to the Court of Cassation is filed. The appeal to the Court of Cassation will not suspend the sentence and no bail will be granted in respect of the sentence by the Court of Appeal.

2.2.3 The Shari'a Courts

The Shari'a or Islamic courts work along side the civil and criminal courts in the UAE.[1] The jurisdiction of the Shari'a court is defined in certain Emirates but not in the Emirates of Abu Dhabi, Sharjah and Ras Al Khaimah.[2] The Shari'a court is the Islamic court in the UAE and is primarily responsible for civil matters in the UAE between Muslims. Non-Muslims will not appear before the Shari'a court in any matter. Shari'a courts have the exclusive jurisdiction to hear certain family matters such as those involving divorce, inheritance, custody, child abuse and guardianship of minors. Shari'a cases are heard by one Judge and the courts apply the UAE codified Law. In the absence of any particular provision in the UAE codified Law,[3] the Islamic principles of Shari'a as found in the Islamic Shari'a textbooks are applied.[4] The Islamic Schools of Shari'a which are applicable in the UAE are the Maliki and the Hambali Schools.[5] Article 1 of the UAE Civil Code[6] provides that if there are no applicable principles in either the Maliki or Hambali Schools, then the Judge must turn to the Shafi School or Hanafi School.[7]

The Shari'a court may, at the Federal level only, (i.e. not in Dubai or Ras Al Khaimah), also hear certain criminal cases such as rape, robbery, driving under the influence of alcohol and related crimes which were originally

---

[1] Dubai Court of Cassation Judgment 19/90 dated 27 January 1991.

[2] Supreme Court of Cassation Judgment 356 for the year 20 dated 12 October 1999.

[3] Supreme Court of Cassation Judgment 20 for the year 16 dated 18 May 1994.

[4] Dubai Court of Cassation Judgment 127/96 dated 19 January 1997.

[5] Dubai Court of Cassation Judgment 24/98 dated 29 November 1998

[6] The Civil Transactions Law, Federal Law No. 5 of 1985, as amended.

[7] Supreme Court of Cassation Judgment 152 for the year 19 dated 6 October 1998.

dealt with in the criminal courts. These matters have been transferred to the Shari'a courts because of the relevance of Shari'a principles to these matters. The Shari'a court will act as a criminal court in these cases and apply the same laws and principles as a criminal court would in accordance with the Criminal Law of Procedure. Further, the Shari'a courts in Abu Dhabi and Ras Al Khaimah have developed the practice of hearing minor civil cases relating to debt recoveries and simple civil disputes between parties. This is an exception to the general rule and there is no guide for such an application under the applicable laws.

2.2.4   The Court of Cassation

The Court of Cassation is the highest court in the UAE and as mentioned, it will only hear matters of law. The Court of Cassation will not only act as an appellate court in respect of the decisions of the lower courts but will also supervise these lower courts and ensure that they are applying and interpreting the law correctly. The Court of Cassation also sets out the principles upon which the lower courts will need to follow and abide.

The UAE has a civil law legal system and therefore the courts do not make law. However, judgments of the Court of Cassation are usually referred to in order to provide guidance on the likely attitude of courts in certain matters and act as a basis for arguments before the courts. Very rarely will Judges of the lower courts contradict the legal principles set out by the Court of Cassation when deciding on a particular case. Judgments of the Court of Cassation are also referred to by lawyers in their pleadings and arguments as a means of persuading the lower courts to rule in their client's favour. The Court of Cassation is the only authority empowered to interpret the codified law and its application to a particular problem.[1]

The Court of Cassation is empowered to overrule or amend any judgment delivered by any lower court.[2] It usually refers the matter back to the Court of Appeal so that the Court of Appeal can review its own decision with regard to the legal principles and guidelines set out by the Court of Cassation. The Court of Cassation usually consists of five Judges. No further evidence will be admissible and the court will usually afford the parties the opportunity to make one written submission and then to argue the case before the court in one hearing before reserving the case for judgment in any civil, criminal or Shari'a matter.

---

[1] Dubai Court of Cassation Judgment 107/2001 dated 5 January 2002.

[2] Dubai Court of Cassation Judgment 63/99 dated 2 May 1999.

There exists an automatic right to appeal any judgment of the Appeal Court whether civil, criminal or Shari'a, to the Court of Cassation irrespective of the amount involved or the crime charged. An appeal to the Court of Cassation does not suspend the execution of a judgment of a lower court,[1] whether civil, criminal or Shari'a unless otherwise ordered by the Court of Cassation in a separate, special application. The judgment of the Court of Cassation will be final and no further appeal is available.

The Emirate of Dubai has its own Court of Cassation that is independent of the Federal courts since the Emirate of Dubai has its own independent court system. In all Emirates other than the Emirates of Dubai and Ras Al Khaimah, the final appeal will be to the Court of Cassation located in Abu Dhabi. Ras Al Khaimah does not have a Court of Cassation and as such the final appellate court in this Emirate is the Court of Appeal.

The Court of Cassation in the Emirate of Dubai applies similar laws and principles to that of the Supreme Court of Cassation with the following exceptions:

1. The Dubai Court of Cassation supervises and acts as an appellate court in relation only to decisions of the lower courts in the Emirate of Dubai.
2. The Dubai Court of Cassation ensures that lower courts in the Emirate of Dubai apply the Federal law of the UAE and the local laws of the Emirate of Dubai.
3. The judgments of the Dubai Court of Cassation have no binding or persuasive effect on the Federal courts of the UAE and their persuasive effect is usually limited to the courts of the Emirate of Dubai. Likewise, decisions of the Supreme Court of Cassation are not usually persuasive in the courts of the Emirate of Dubai.

Only the Supreme Court of Cassation may determine a Federal constitutional matter and those matters set out in the UAE Constitution (irrespective of the Emirate involved). The Supreme Court of Cassation also has the exclusive role of adjudicating upon any dispute between one Emirate and another.

Normally, the decisions of the Dubai Court of Cassation and the Supreme Court of Cassation are coherent and are uniform on most matters. There have, however, been some contradictions between the decisions of the two courts in interpreting particular laws or their application to certain facts and circumstances.

---

[1] Dubai Court of Appeal Judgment 723/97 dated 7 August 1997.

2.2.5 Special Tribunals

In exceptional circumstances, the Ruler of an Emirate or the Minister of Justice upon the direction of the Ruler may form a special committee to hear and look into a particular dispute to adjudicate matters or to look into all claims made in connection with a matter.[1] This is usually done on a local level and in exceptional cases such as large family disputes or a complicated bankruptcy matter. The committee will be headed either by a Judge or a non-Judge and its decision is final, binding and not subject to appeal.

2.3   Court Fees

The amount of court fees differ from one Emirate to another.[2] Court fees and the structure of court charges are stipulated by Federal Decree No. 15 of 1992 which applies to the Federal courts and Law No. 1 of 1994 which applies only to the Dubai Court. Ras Al Khaimah has its own regulations for the payment of court fees in accordance with the Court Ordinance of 1971.

Normally, the court will make an order regarding the payment of court fees upon delivery of the judgment, the general rule being that the losing party will be ordered to pay the court fees.[3] It is unlikely that the court will grant an exemption or deferral from the payment of court fees.[4] However, in very limited circumstances, such as where personal injuries are involved, the court may grant an exemption. Once the court fees are paid into court it is not possible to obtain a refund even in the event that the action is withdrawn or a settlement is reached between the parties.[5]

In addition to court fees there may be other costs involved such as translation costs. The court will only accept translations from duly licensed translators[6] and it is likely that both the claimant and the defendant will

---

[1] Dubai Court of Cassation Judgment 110/99 dated 29 May 1999.

[2] See Appendix 1.

[3] Supreme Court of Cassation Judgment 277 for the year 16 dated 17 March 1999. Dubai Court of Cassation Judgment 300/91 dated 23 February 1992.

[4] Dubai Court of Cassation Judgment 223/90 dated 4 May 1991.

[5] Dubai Court of Cassation Judgment 23/90 dated 14 May 1990.

[6] Supreme Court of Cassation Judgment 120 and 132 for the year 20 dated 29 February 2000.

incur translation expenses. Translation charges are not recoverable, even if the substantive claim succeeds.[1]

If an expert is appointed, it is likely that the court will order both parties to share his fees, the amount of which depends on the complexity of the issue and the expert himself.

---

[1] Dubai Court of Appeal Judgment 723/97 dated 7 August 1997.

Chapter Three

JURISDICTION AND FORUM

Prior to filing a claim, a potential litigant should ensure that the UAE courts and the courts of the Emirate concerned, whether Federal or local, have jurisdiction to hear the dispute. An action filed against persons or companies domiciled in the UAE will be governed by the Civil Procedure Law, which law governs jurisdiction of all UAE courts including the courts within the Emirates of Dubai and Ras Al Khaimah. Any action must be filed before the courts in the relevant Emirate having jurisdiction, failing which the court may dismiss the action on the grounds that it has no jurisdiction to hear the matter.

3.1   International Jurisdiction

International jurisdiction relates to when the courts of the UAE in general (as opposed to the individual courts of each Emirate) have jurisdiction over an action with an international element. For example, the UAE courts will have jurisdiction with regard to any action which is filed against a UAE national and will have jurisdiction over a foreign person or entity who is domiciled in the UAE. The only exception relates to actions involving real estate property situated outside the UAE.

International jurisdiction is a matter of public policy and therefore the court may dismiss the action for lack of jurisdiction even if the defendant fails to raise the issue and even if the defendant is not present.[1] Any arguments relating to the jurisdiction of the court, because it is a matter of public policy, may be raised before the Court of First Instance, Court of Appeal or Cassation, that is, at any stage and at any time during the proceedings.[2]

---

[1] Article 23 of the Civil Procedure Law.

[2] Article 85 of the Civil Procedure Law.

The Civil Procedure Law provides certain criteria for determining whether a UAE court will have jurisdiction in a case which has either an international element or filed against a foreign person or entity.

The UAE courts shall have jurisdiction to deal with any claim raised against a citizen of the UAE and against a foreign person or entity which has a domicile or place of residence in the UAE.[1] Furthermore, the courts will have jurisdiction over a foreign person or entity which has no domicile or residence in the UAE[2] under the following circumstances:

1. If he has chosen a domicile in the UAE;[3]
2. If the action relates to assets located in the UAE or to an inheritance to be distributed in the UAE;[4]
3. If the action relates to a contract or obligation which was executed, entered into or implemented in full or part in the UAE; or in connection with a contract which was notarised in the UAE; or relates to an incident that took place in the UAE; or to a bankruptcy which has been declared by the UAE courts;[5]
4. If the action is filed by a wife who is domiciled in the UAE against her husband who was previously domiciled in the UAE;[6]
5. If the action relates to alimony or custody or guardianship where the wife, minor or the guardian is in the UAE;[7]
6. If the action relates to personal status and the claimant is a UAE national or a foreign person or entity who is domiciled in the UAE and the defendant has no known address outside the UAE or if the UAE law is the applicable law;[8]

---

[1] Article 20 of the Civil Procedure Law. Dubai Court of Cassation Judgment 353/98 dated 21 November 1998.

[2] Article 21 of the Civil Procedure Law. Dubai Court of Cassation Judgment 155/97 dated 8 June 1997.

[3] Article 21(1) of the Civil Procedure Law. Dubai Court of Cassation Judgment 509/99 dated 29 April 2000.

[4] Article 21(2) of the Civil Procedure Law. Supreme Court of Cassation Judgment 227 for the year 17 dated 28 January 1996, Supreme Court of Cassation Judgment 301 for the year 17 dated 9 June 1996

[5] Article 21(3) of the Civil Procedure Law. Dubai Court of Cassation Judgment dated 166/95 dated 11 February 1996, Supreme Court of Cassation Judgment 318 for the year 18 dated 12 November 1996, Supreme Court of Cassation Judgment 482 for the year 18 dated 15 April 1997, Supreme Court of Cassation Judgment 396 for the year 20 dated 26 September 2000.

[6] Article 21(4) of the Civil Procedure Law. Dubai Court of Cassation Judgment 42/2001 dated 18 November 2001.

[7] Article 21(5) of the Civil Procedure Law.

[8] Article 21(6) of the Civil Procedure Law. Supreme Court of Cassation Judgment 307 for the year 16 dated 17 December 1995.

7. If one of the defendants in the action has a domicile or place of residence in the UAE.[1]

3.2 Domestic Jurisdiction

Domestic ("local") jurisdiction refers to the jurisdiction of the courts of the individual Emirates to hear an action. For instance, once it has been determined that the UAE has jurisdiction in respect of an action, one must turn to domestic jurisdiction to determine in which particular Emirate the action must be filed. This is not a matter of public policy and the party concerned must raise such a defence before the court.

If the defendant, or one of the defendants is domiciled in the UAE, the following factors will be considered in determining whether the courts of a particular Emirate will have jurisdiction:

1. The claim must be filed with the court in whose geographical area the defendant's domicile is located. If the defendant has no domicile in the state, the claim should be filed in the courts of the Emirate in which the defendant is resident or employed.[2]
2. The claim may be filed with the court which has jurisdiction over the place in which the damage has occurred in actions for damages caused to persons or property.[3]
3. Commercial matters should be heard by the court having jurisdiction over the place where the defendant is domiciled or the place where the agreement was concluded or executed, in full or in part, or where the agreement was meant to have been implemented.[4]
4. In cases involving several defendants, the court having jurisdiction over the domicile of any one of them shall be the appropriate court in which to file the claim.[5]
5. In actions against companies, associations and other private entities, jurisdiction will be accorded to the court having jurisdiction over the

---

[1] Article 21(7) of the Civil Procedure Law. Dubai Court of Cassation Judgment 9/93 dated 16 May 1993.

[2] Article 31(1) of the Civil Procedure Law. Dubai Court of Cassation Judgment 486/99 dated 30 April 2000.

[3] Article 31(2) of the Civil Procedure Law. Supreme Court of Cassation Judgment 300 for the year 18 dated 30 September 1997.

[4] Article 31(3) of the Civil Procedure Law. Supreme Court of Cassation Judgment 290 for the year 17 dated 28 November 1995, Supreme Court of Cassation Judgment 585 for the year 18 dated 31 March 1996, Supreme Court of Cassation Judgment 81 for the year 17 dated 16 March 1997.

[5] Article 31(4) of the Civil Procedure Law. Supreme Court of Cassation Judgment 444 for the year 18 dated 6 May 1997.

place in which the head office is located. An action may, however, be filed with the court having jurisdiction over the place in which a branch office is located, provided the claim relates to the branch office.[1]

6. Actions for the distribution of an inheritance shall be filed with the court having jurisdiction over the last place in which the deceased was domiciled.[2]

7. Cases involving commercial insolvency shall be filed with the court having jurisdiction over the place in which the commercial entity is located. If the commercial entity has more than one place of business, the court having jurisdiction over the place in which the head office is located shall have jurisdiction.[3]

8. Claims involving supplies, contracting, rents payable for housing and employee's remuneration should be filed with the court having jurisdiction over the place in which the defendant is domiciled or where the agreement was concluded or executed.[4]

9. Insurance policy claims should be filed with the court having jurisdiction over the place in which the beneficiaries are domiciled or where the insured goods are or were situated.[5]

Finally, where the defendant does not have a place of domicile in the UAE and it is not possible to appoint a court of jurisdiction in accordance with the rules outlined above, an action may be filed with the court having jurisdiction over the claimant's place of domicile. In the event that the claimant does not have a place of domicile in the UAE, the action must be filed in the Federal court in Abu Dhabi.[6]

---

[1] Article 33 of the Civil Procedure Law. Dubai Court of Cassation Judgment 174/98 dated 30 May 1998.

[2] Article 34 of the Civil Procedure Law. Supreme Court of Cassation Judgment 168 for the year 21 dated 28 September 1999.

[3] Article 35 of the Civil Procedure Law.

[4] Article 36 of the Civil Procedure Law.

[5] Article 37 of the Civil Procedure Law. Dubai Court of Cassation Judgment 176/96 dated 8 March 1997, Supreme Court of Cassation Judgment 247 for the year 21 dated 20 December 2000.

[6] Article 40 of the Civil Procedure Law. Supreme Court of Cassation Judgment 116 for the year dated 13 April 1993.

3.3   Jurisdiction Over Property

3.3.1   Real Estate and Granted Land

Actions relating to a dispute over real estate matters must be filed before the court which has jurisdiction over the place in which the real estate property is situated. Claims for money relating to real estate must be filed with the court having jurisdiction over the place in which the real estate is situated or where the defendant is domiciled.[1] This is a matter of public policy and the parties may not agree otherwise.

Furthermore, the court will only entertain an action filed in connection with real estate property and not in respect of granted land. A dispute relating to ownership or any title over granted land may only be heard before a court in the UAE by order of the Lands Department or by decree of the Ruler in each individual Emirate. Granted land is usually gifted by the government to an individual or entity and therefore the full title of the property remains in the hands of the government.

In Dubai, in addition to the above rules, any action with regard to real estate property may not be filed before the court unless the claimant has a letter from the Dubai Lands Department referring the action to the courts. This rule relates to full title property (real estate property) and any action relating to a dispute over the ownership or any right over the property.[2]

3.3.2   Movable Property

The UAE courts do not have jurisdiction over movable property (whether it consists of goods, materials or a vessel), by virtue of the fact that the movable property is located in the UAE, if it has no jurisdiction on the merits.

However, in terms of judgments of the Dubai Court of Cassation, it may be possible to obtain an order for attachment even if the UAE courts have no jurisdiction on the merits or if the parties have agreed to foreign arbitration

---

[1] Article 32 of the Civil Procedure Law. Dubai Court of Cassation Judgment 403/99 dated 20 March 1999.

[2] Dubai Court of Cassation Judgment 1/95 dated 14 October 1995, Dubai Court of Cassation Judgment 447/98 dated 6 March 1999.

in the relevant agreement.[1] This is provided that, following the attachment, the claimant provides evidence that he has initiated an action in the foreign jurisdiction concerned or has proceeded with the arbitration proceedings in accordance with the agreement.

"Arrest for security only" pending judgment in foreign proceedings, whilst possible in terms of the Civil Procedure Law, is not well established in practice in the UAE, and remains an uncertain area of law.

Also, according to Article 122 of the UAE Maritime Code,[2] the UAE courts will have jurisdiction to arrest a vessel if one of the conditions contained in Article 122 thereof is fulfilled, in addition to the rules on international and domestic jurisdiction referred to above and set out in the Civil Procedure Law.

Article 122 of the Maritime Code reads as follows:

The civil court within the area of which the arrest is effected shall have jurisdiction to adjudicate upon the subject matter of the claim in the following circumstances, even if the vessel does not have the nationality of the State, in addition to those circumstances set out in the procedural laws in force in the State:

1. *If the claimant has a usual place of residence or head office in the state.*
2. *If the maritime debt arose in the State.*
3. *If the maritime debt arose during a voyage during which the arrest was effected on the vessel.*
4. *If the maritime debt arose out of a collision or assistance over which the court has jurisdiction.*
5. *If the debt is secured by a maritime mortgage over the arrested vessel.*

In summary, the fact that goods or property of a defendant is located in an Emirate does not grant a court jurisdiction over the matter in dispute even if the dispute is related to this property, unless the court had jurisdiction over the matter according to the jurisdiction rules set out above.

---

[1] Dubai Court of Cassation Judgment 283/94 dated 28 May 1995, Dubai Court of Cassation Judgment 194/95 dated 9 March 1996.

[2] Federal Law No. 26 of 1981.

3.4 Jurisdiction in Respect of Subject Matter

3.4.1 Labour Jurisdiction

Under the UAE Federal Labour Law,[1] all disputes involving labour actions filed in court must also be filed with the Dispute Resolution Office of the Ministry of Labour and Social Affairs. If the action is filed before a court without being referred to the Ministry of Labour and Social Affairs the civil court will dismiss the action.

The Dispute Resolution Office of the Ministry of Labour and Social Affairs is not a court and will not act as a judicial authority in determining the matter. It is a forum for dispute resolution and it tries to mediate between the employer and the employee to settle the matter. The Ministry of Labour and Social Affairs encourages the parties to settle their dispute amicably.[2] If the dispute is not settled within ten days following a formal complaint filed by either party, the Ministry of Labour and Social Affairs will transfer the matter to the civil court together with a formal document from the Ministry of Labour and Social Affairs requesting the court to proceed with the action.

Labour matters will be heard by the same civil court as any other commercial and civil matter in terms of the Civil Procedure Law but will usually progress more quickly than a normal commercial or civil action.

3.4.2 Rent Disputes

The courts in the Emirates of Dubai, Sharjah and Ajman do not exercise jurisdiction over rent disputes. In accordance with certain local decrees issued in each of these Emirates, disputes involving landlord and tenant fall within the jurisdiction of a rent committee seated at the municipality in the individual Emirate concerned.[3]

---

[1] Federal Law No. 8 of 1980, as amended, (the Labour Law), Dubai Court of Cassation Judgment 65/98 and 114/98 dated 31 May 1998, Supreme Court of Cassation Judgment 417 for the year 19 dated 22 June 1999.

[2] Article 155(4) of the Federal Law No. 8 of 1980 as amended.

[3] Dubai Court of Cassation Judgment 82/93 dated 10 July 1993, Dubai Court of Cassation Judgment 375/98 dated 15 November 1998, Dubai Court of Cassation Judgment 194/98 dated 26 December 1998.

The rent committee will adjudicate any dispute arising between landlord and tenant and deliver a judgment on the matter, which will be executed in court. The rent committees do not follow the provisions of the Civil Procedure Law in its form, substance or procedure. It is rather a declaration determining the outcome of a dispute between the parties which can be executed in court immediately. A rent committee usually consists of a number of prominent businessmen from the community in the Emirate concerned, together with a legal adviser (who is often the legal adviser of the Municipality) to assist them on legal matters.

In Sharjah,[1] awards in claims not exceeding AED 100,000 shall be final and not subject to appeal or review. A complaint against an award for an amount exceeding AED 100,000 may be forwarded to a Complaints Committee within 15 days from the date of issue of the award if the parties are present or within 15 days from the date that the debtor was notified thereof. The Complaints Committee consists of three Judges nominated by the Minister of Justice and holds office at the Municipality. The Chairman of the Committee is required to be a Judge appointed by the Minister of Justice and Islamic Affairs.[2] Nominal fees are payable to the rent committee for deciding a rent dispute.

In Dubai, the Dubai Rents Committee was established by Decree No. 2 of 1993, regarding the formation of a special Judicial Committee for Reconciliation of disputes between Tenants and Landlords, which provided for the establishment of an Executive Committee which has the exclusive authority to consider all disputes between landlord and tenant in Dubai. The Committees award is final and is not subject to appeal or review.

3.4.3 Administrative Jurisdiction

Administrative disputes are generally disputes between the private sector and the government over a contractual matter or in respect of a tortious action. Unlike other civil jurisdiction countries, the UAE does not have an administrative court to deal with administrative disputes and administrative actions are heard by the civil court. Thus, all administrative actions filed by the government or by the private sector against the government may be filed before the court in the normal way and the action will be governed by the Civil Procedure Law. Actions filed against the Federal Government must

---

[1] Article 5/B of Law No. 6 for 2001 organising the Relationship between Landlord and Tenant in the Emirate of Sharjah.

[2] Article 4/1 of Law No. 6 for 2001 organising the Relationship between Landlord and Tenant in the Emirate of Sharjah.

however be filed before the Federal courts according to the rules of jurisdiction provided above.[1]

An action filed against local government departments in the Emirate of Dubai or Ras Al Khaimah must be filed before the courts in the individual Emirate concerned. It is not possible to file an action against the local government departments of the Emirate of Dubai or Ras Al Khaimah before the Federal court. Similarly, the Dubai or Ras Al Khaimah courts will not entertain an action filed against the Federal Government.

In Dubai, an action against the Government of Dubai or any of its entities may not be filed in court without obtaining the prior consent of the Ruler's Court.[2] This involves an application to the legal advisor of the Ruler requesting a consent to file an action against the government. After having reviewed the application, leave is usually granted by the Ruler. Once the leave is obtained an action may be filed in court in the normal way.[3]

Claims by the government of the individual Emirates require no consent from the Ruler. In Dubai, such claims are made by the Attorney General or a lawyer who has been deputed to act on his behalf. The Attorney General usually represents the government in protecting its interests or pursuing a claim. In the other Emirates and in respect of cases involving the Federal Government, the Department of Al Fatwa and Al Tashrie will represent the respective Emirates or the Federal Government as the case may be.

3.4.4 Jurisdiction over Free Zones

Many free zones have been established in the UAE and the number is growing. These free zones allow foreign corporations 100% ownership of their business and are characterised by a flexible approach to encourage investment. Courts in the UAE have jurisdiction over matters that arise in the free zone areas.

---

[1] Supreme Court of Cassation Judgment 65 for the year 4 dated 1 March 1983, Supreme Court of Cassation Judgment 17 for the year 7 dated 19 January 1992, Supreme Court of Cassation Judgment 116 for the year 14 dated 13 April 1993, Supreme Court of Cassation Judgment 18 for the year 17 dated 6 June 1995.

[2] Instructions Regarding Government Cases in the Emirate of Dubai issued by the Ruler of Dubai on 2 July 1992 and Dubai Law No. 4 of 1997.

[3] Dubai Court of Cassation Judgment 32/94 dated 26 June 1994, Dubai Court of Cassation Judgment 110/96 dated 29 December 1996.

The jurisdiction of the court in each Emirate concerned will extend to the free zone areas within that Emirate, and will apply the applicable free zone law as well as any other general law that may be applicable to the free zone areas within that Emirate. There is no separate judicial jurisdiction for the free zone areas. In general, the Constitution, and all laws, regulations and decrees that are applicable in the Emirate in which the free zone is located, will apply to the free zone areas except for those laws, regulations and decrees which are specifically excluded by virtue of the free zone law.

Free Zones

- Ajman Free Zone
- Dubai Airport Free Zone (DAFZA)
- Dubai Cars and Automobile Free Zone
- Dubai Technology, E-Commerce and Media Free Zone (Dubai Internet City, Dubai Media City, Dubai Knowledge Village)
- Fujairah Free Trade Zone
- Dubai Gold and Diamond Park
- Jebel Ali Free Zone (JAFZA)
- Sharjah Hamriyah Free Zone
- Sharjah Airport Free Zone
- Ras Al Khaimah Free Zone
- Um Al Quwain Free Zone

3.5 Choice of Forum

The UAE does not recognise the choice of forum or the forum non-convenience principle. As such the courts will not assume jurisdiction on the grounds that the parties have agreed to give the court of a particular Emirate jurisdiction to hear the matter.[1] The UAE courts (including the courts of the Emirates of Ras Al Khaimah and Dubai) will only hear the matter if they have jurisdiction to hear the dispute based on the criteria set out above or as provided for in Article 122 of the Maritime Code referred to above. This is true even if the parties have agreed to have their dispute heard in the UAE.

The same rule applies within the UAE between the UAE Emirates. In other words a party in Abu Dhabi may not agree to give the jurisdiction to a Dubai court if the latter has no jurisdiction over the matter in the first place and hence the action filed in Dubai will be dismissed.[2]

3.6 Choice of Law

There are no provisions in the UAE laws providing for the right of parties to agree on the choice of law other than the following:

a) Article 19 of the UAE Civil Code, Federal Law No. 5 of 1985, reads as follows:

  (i) *The form and the substance of contractual obligations shall be governed by the law of the state in which the contracting parties are both resident if they are resident in the same state, but if they are resident in different states, the law of the state in which the contract was concluded shall apply unless they agree, or it is apparent from the circumstances that the intention was, that another law should apply.*[3]

  (ii) *The lex situs of the place in which the real property is situated shall apply to contracts made over such property.*[4]

---

[1] Dubai Court of Cassation Judgment 265/94 dated 8 January 1995.

[2] Supreme Court of Cassation Judgment 137 for the year 11 dated 21 January 1990, Dubai Court of Cassation Judgment 333/94 dated 26 March 1995, Supreme Court of Cassation Judgment 255 for the year 17 dated 9 June 1996, Dubai Court of Cassation Judgment 154/97 dated 22 November 1997, Dubai Court of Cassation Judgment 136/2000 dated 26 November 2000.

[3] Supreme Court of Cassation Judgment 240 for the year 13 dated 23 June 1992.

[4] Supreme Court of Cassation Judgment 92 for the year 6 dated 28 April 1985.

b) Provisions in the UAE Civil law which deal with the application of foreign family law by statutory order.

There are also no laws in the UAE which deal with the complicated nature of the conflict of laws when it comes to application. In principle the law in the UAE recognises the parties' autonomy for the choice of law clause, however, in practice (with the exception of family law matters[1]) it is almost impossible to apply foreign law to a transaction in connection with an action heard before the UAE court. In most cases, the courts in the UAE will apply the local law and will have little or no regard to the foreign law in the absence of evidence provided by the parties of the provisions of the foreign law to which they have agreed.

The courts in the UAE presume that it is the duty of the party seeking to apply a foreign law to provide the court with adequate evidence of the provisions of the relevant law upon which he is relying.[2] In practice, the court will often apply the local law to the substance of the matter even if the parties have agreed on a foreign law to be the governing law of the contract.

In the light of the above, whenever the parties intend to agree on a foreign law to be the governing law of the contract, they would be advised to agree to proceed to arbitration rather than to the courts to ensure the application of the foreign law. In such instances, the court will uphold the arbitration award (provided it is within the criteria required) under the law including the foreign law which was applied in the arbitration proceedings.[3]

The UAE does have reciprocal agreements with the GCC states, France and India and co-operative arrangements with Syria, Egypt, Jordan, Tunisia, Algeria, Sudan, Somalia, Djibouti, Palestine, Lebanon, Libya, Morocco, Mauritania and Yemen.[4] However, the UAE is not a party to any international treaty, convention or other reciprocal agreement which may give any special treatment to any particular country for the application of foreign law.

---

[1] Dubai Court of Cassation Judgment 20/95 dated 15 June 1996.

[2] Dubai Court of Cassation Judgment 467/98 and 11/99 dated 28 February 1999, Dubai Court of Cassation Judgment 19/99 dated 31 October 1999, Dubai Court of Cassation Judgment 17/2001 dated 10 March 2001.

[3] Dubai Court of Cassation Judgment 240/2001 dated 8 December 2001.

[4] See Appendix 2.

3.7 Enforcement of Foreign Judgments

The enforcement of foreign judgments is regulated by Articles 235 and 236 of the Civil Procedure Law. Enforcement of foreign judgments in the UAE is provided for in principle, made acceptable and possible, although the applicable conditions may be difficult to apply.[1] Thus foreign judgments may be enforced in the UAE if they satisfy the following conditions:

Article 235

1. *Judgments and orders issued in a foreign country may be ordered to be enforced in the State of the United Arab Emirates on the same conditions as prescribed in the laws of that country for the enforcement and similar judgments and orders issued in the State.*

2. *An enforcement order shall be applied for under normal litigation procedures to the Court of First Instance within whose jurisdiction the enforcement is required. Enforcement may not be ordered until the following has been verified:*

   a) *The State Courts do not have jurisdiction in the dispute in which the judgment has been given or the order made, and that the foreign Courts which issued it have jurisdiction therein under the international rules for legal jurisdiction prescribed in their laws.*
   b) *That the judgment or order has been issued by a Court having jurisdiction under the law of the country in which issued.*
   c) *That the opposing parties in the case in which the foreign judgment has been given have been summoned to appear, and have duly appeared.*
   d) *That the judgment or order has acquired the force of an accomplished fact under the law of the Court which issued it.*
   e) *That it does not conflict with a judgment or order previously issued by a Court in the State and contains nothing in breach of public morals or order in the State.*

Article 236

The provisions of the foregoing Article shall apply to the rulings of arbitrators issued in a foreign country. An arbitrator's ruling must have been given in a matter which may be arbitrated under the State laws and must be enforceable in the country in which it is issued.

---

[1] Dubai Court of Cassation Judgment 117/93 dated 20 November 1993, Dubai Court of Cassation Judgment 286/97 dated 14 March 1998, Supreme Court of Cassation Judgment 503 for the year 21 dated 24 June 2001.

The enforcement of a foreign judgment in the UAE is by way of an application to court, filed in the same manner as a normal action, requesting the court to ratify the foreign judgment (unless otherwise provided by special treaty or bilateral agreement) for execution in the UAE. Upon submitting the application to the court the claimant must pay the necessary court fees and provide the court with the following:

1. A copy of the foreign judgment duly notarised and authenticated by the UAE embassy in the country where the judgment originated, along with a certified Arabic translation.
2. Evidence that the judgment is final and that no further appeal is applicable or possible, again duly authorised and authenticated by the UAE Embassy in the country where the judgment originated along with a certified Arabic translation.
3. Evidence that the defendant was properly represented in the case and that summons was properly served on him.
4. Evidence that the judgment is final and good for enforcement in its form in the country where the judgment was delivered and that it is good for execution and no further appeal is possible.[1]
5. Evidence that the country where the judgment originated has a reciprocal arrangement for the enforcement of UAE judgments in that country. This evidence is usually provided by way of an affidavit or other evidence, to show that the country where the judgment was issued would enforce a UAE judgment in similar circumstances. Such evidence must be duly notarised and authenticated by the UAE embassy in the country where the judgment originated together with a certified Arabic translation.

It is important not only to consider the requirements of the UAE law but also to ensure that the court in the foreign jurisdiction complied fully with the requirements of the UAE law relating to the enforcement of foreign judgments during the hearing of the case. For example, it is important that if service of summons took place, that the summons not only satisfied the requirements under that jurisdiction but also meets the minimum criteria required under UAE law. The UAE courts may not enforce a foreign judgment if the Judge is of the opinion that the service of summons was not properly conducted or does not meet the standards required.

Finally, it is important for the enforcement of foreign judgments that the UAE court did not have jurisdiction in the first place. If it becomes evident at the time the judgment is filed for enforcement in the UAE that the UAE

---

[1] Dubai Court of Cassation Judgment 267/99 dated 27 November 1999.

courts had jurisdiction over the subject matter of the dispute, the UAE courts will not enforce the foreign judgment.[1]

3.8 Treaties

The UAE has ratified a number of reciprocal treaties in recent years including the Gulf Co-Operation Council Treaty,[2] the Bilateral Treaty for the Enforcement of Judgments with France,[3] the Agreement between the UAE and India on Juridical and Judicial Co-operation in Civil and Commercial matters.[4] It has also entered into certain co-operative arrangements with other countries[5] including Jordan,[6] Morocco,[7] Saudi Arabia,[8] Syria,[9] Somalia,[10] Algeria[11] and Egypt.[12]

Notwithstanding the existence of these reciprocal treaties and co-operative arrangements, it is not easy to enforce foreign judgments in the UAE. Even the existing treaties pose difficulties because of the conditions contained therein and the powers given to judicial authorities to look into those conditions and to evaluate them. Nevertheless, the provisions of the treaty will be applied before local law.[13]

3.8.1 Gulf Co-Operation Council Convention

The UAE, Bahrain, Qatar, Kuwait, the Kingdom of Saudi Arabia, Sultanate of Oman, being the six members of the Gulf Co-operation Council States (the "GCC"), signed and ratified a regional treaty for the enforcement of judgments delivered in any of the six states. The GCC Convention for the Enforcement of Judgments and Judicial Notices and Delegations was signed

---

[1] Dubai Court of Cassation Judgment 117/93 dated 20 November 1993.
[2] Federal Decree No. 41 of 1996.
[3] Federal Decree No. 31 of 1992.
[4] Federal Decree No. 33 of 2000.
[5] See Appendix 2.
[6] Federal Decree No. 106 of 1999.
[7] Federal Decree No. 80 of 1978.
[8] The "Al Riyadh Agreement" Federal Decree No.53 of 1999.
[9] Federal Decree No. 12 of 1980.
[10] Federal Decree No.95 of 1982.
[11] Federal Decree No.12 of 1984.
[12] Federal Decree No.83 of 2000.
[13] Supreme Court of Cassation Judgment 236 for the year 19 dated 14 April 1998.

by members of the GCC Council and ratified by the UAE on 17 June 1996 by Federal Decree No. 41 of 1996. The Convention provides for the following:

1. Each member state of the GCC shall execute civil and commercial judgments as well as judgments given on family matters of the other members of the GCC, according to the procedures set out in the Treaty, provided that the court which has issued the decision has jurisdiction and provided that the court where the application is made to execute the judgment has jurisdiction to execute the judgment.
2. The application to execute the judgment must be accompanied by a copy of the judgment together with any decision made by the court.
3. An application for the execution of the judgment will be denied if:

   a) it is contrary to the Shari'a principles, the Constitution or the public policy of the country where the application was made;
   b) the judgment was a default judgment and the defendant was not properly summoned;
   c) the judgment contradicts a judgment delivered from the local court where the application was made to execute the judgment;
   d) the subject matter of the application is being litigated before the court where the application is made to be executed;
   e) the judgment was delivered against the government of the country concerned or one of the employees of the government concerned by virtue of him executing his job as a government employee;
   f) the judgment contradicts any agreement or treaties entered into by the country where the application is made to execute the judgment.

The court where the application is made to execute the judgment only has jurisdiction to ratify the execution of the judgment and may not look into the merits of the case. The application is accordingly made directly to the execution court to enforce the judgment.

The GCC Convention also deals with applications made by one state to another to assign another state to enforce a judgment or deal with procedures such as the calling of witnesses, service of summons, inspections or any other jurisdiction procedures which can be implemented by petition. Applications may be made directly from one court to another, without having to go through the diplomatic channels.

The GCC Convention simplifies the enforcement of judgments between the GCC States. It is now possible for any member state of the GCC to enforce judgments in any of the GCC States if the above criteria are fulfilled without having to go through all the criteria required in for the enforcement of foreign judgments under the UAE Civil Procedure Law.

Articles 2 and 4 of the GCC Convention do however give rise to difficulties in enforcement as the judicial authority may interfere in the judgment. While in principle judgments delivered in the GCC States can be enforced in another GCC State through a normal enforcement procedure (as opposed to filing a civil case in the country where the judgment is intended to be enforced), the practice is however currently rather vague. The applicant may have to file an action through the normal course of action for enforcement of a judgment in a GCC State, despite the provisions of the convention.

Articles 2 and 4 of the Convention read as follows:

Article 2

The execution of judgment can be rejected totally or partially in the following cases:
1. *If it is contrary to Islamic Shari'a laws, or the provisions of the Constitution, or the public order in the state where execution is required.*
2. *If it was in absentia and the defendant was not properly summoned to the hearing or to the judgment.*
3. *If the dispute in which the judgment was delivered is the same in which a previous judgment was delivered between the same parties and relates to the same matter and cause of action and having the effect of an adjudicated matter in the state which is required to execute or in another member to the Treaty.*
4. *If the dispute in which the judgment was delivered is the subject of a case under deliberation in any of the Courts of the state which is required to execute, and which relates to the same matter and same cause of action, and that such case was filed prior to the filing of the case in the state in which judgment was delivered.*
5. *If the judgment was delivered against the government of the state which is required to execute or against one of its employees due to work undertaken during his employment or as a result of it.*
6. *If the execution of the judgment is contrary to international treaties and agreements applied in the state which is required to execute.*

Article 4

In issues not stipulated in Articles 5 and 6 of this treaty, the Courts of the state in which the judgment was delivered are to be considered competent in the following cases:
1. *If the domicile of the defendant or his place of stay at the time of the opening of the case is in the territory of the state.*
2. *If at the time of opening the case, the defendant has a business or a branch in the territory of the state and the dispute related to the performance or activity of this business or branch.*
3. *If the contractual obligation, the matter of dispute was executed or executory in this state.*
4. *In the event of non-contractual liability if the act of liability occurred in the territory of this state.*
5. *If the respondent has accepted openly the competency of the Courts of the state either by specification of a chosen domicile or by agreement whenever the law of this state does not prohibit such agreement.*
6. *If the respondent has presented his defence in the case without arguing the lack of competency of the Court before which the dispute was filed.*

3.8.2 Bilateral Treaty for the Enforcement of Judgments with France

In terms of Decree No. 31 of 1992 dated 27th of April 1992, the UAE government ratified the Judicial Co-operation and Recognition of Judgments in Civil and Commercial matters between the United Arab Emirates and the Republic of France. It is now possible to enforce judgments delivered by French courts in the UAE and vice-versa, subject to the following conditions:

1. The Treaty has prescribed procedures in which any notices can be executed and forwarded from the one country to the other to be enforced or executed in the other country.
2. In executing service or calling on witness, the country where the procedure has been implemented will apply its own procedure, however, the country which is applying for the service to be implemented may request such implementation or execution in a different manner provided that such manner is not contrary to public policy.
3. No fees will be charged for executing a petition, summons or calling of witness unless a fee is to be paid to an expert or in case there is a fee payable for executing the deputation or the request in a special manner.

In terms of the Treaty, an arbitration award or a judgment delivered in the UAE or France, will be executable and enforceable in the other jurisdiction if:

1. The judgment is delivered by a judicial authority which has jurisdiction.
2. According to the principles of public international law.
3. The judgment is final and is not subject to any appeal.
4. Both parties were properly summoned and were represented or considered to be *in absentia*.
5. That the judgment is not contrary to public policy.
6. It is not in conflict with the judgment delivered by country where the application was made to enforce the award nor is there a case which has been filed prior to the foreign judgment and is still in the process of being litigated.
7. The judgment will not be reviewed by the local court where the application was made to execute the judgment. The court will only apply the law of procedure to enforce the judgment and will not consider the merits of the case.

The official full text of the judgment, the original notice given by the parties inviting them to attend the hearing and anything equivalent to the same, evidence of the fact that the party has been summoned but failed to attend the proceeding or any equivalent document of the same and any evidence to show that the judgment is final and is not subject to any further appeal, must be accompany the application to enforce the judgment. All these documents must be translated, notarised and authenticated.

All the above will apply to an arbitration award provided that the party also encloses evidence of the agreement in terms of which the parties have agreed to refer the dispute to arbitration and the subject matter of the arbitration may be arbitrated.

This treaty is considered to be a marked improvement over the previous practice in the UAE and has greatly simplified the enforcement of foreign judgments in the UAE. It also has been confirmed that service of summons and the procedural aspects of a case before judgment, is a matter of French Law, and not that of the UAE courts. Accordingly, the UAE Judge will not interfere in the procedure of the case before judgment other than to satisfy that the judgment meets the conditions of the treaty.[1]

---

[1] Supreme Court of Cassation Judgment 41 for the year 17 dated 12 April 1998.

3.8.3 Reciprocal Agreement between the UAE and India

A reciprocal enforcement agreement between the UAE and India signed in New Delhi on 25 October 1999 entitled "The Agreement between the Government of the United Arab Emirates and the Government of the Republic of India on Juridical and Judicial Co-operation in Civil and Commercial matters for the service of Summons, Judicial Documents, Judicial Commissions, Execution of Judgments and Arbitral Awards." This Agreement was ratified by the UAE by Federal Decree dated 29 March 2000 and was subsequently published in the Official Gazette.[1]

Article I states under "scope of application" that the Agreement applies to the execution of decrees, settlements and arbitral awards. Article XV states that each of the contracting parties shall, in accordance with its laws, recognise and/ or execute decrees passed by the courts of the other contracting party in civil, commercial and personal matters and by criminal courts in civil matters. Article XV (2) states that the term "decree" as used in the Agreement, whatever its designation, means any decisions rendered in judicial proceedings by a competent court of the contracting states.

Article XVIII states that in matters other than capacity or status of a person or immovable property, the courts of a contracting party shall have jurisdiction, amongst others, in the following cases:

1. if the defendant has its domicile or residence in the territory of that state at the time of institution of the suit;
2. if the defendant has, at the time of instituting the suit, a place or a branch in the territory; or
3. by an express or implied agreement between the plaintiff and the defendant, the contractual obligations giving rise to the litigation are or have to be performed in the territory of the state.

Article XXII (1) states that the competent judicial authority in the state requested to recognise or execute a decree shall without reviewing the merits of the case, confine itself to ascertaining the compliance of the decree with the conditions provided for in the Agreement. The procedure for this is set out in Article XXIII, which states that the central authority of the contracting party requesting recognition or execution of a decree in the other contracting party shall submit the following:

---

[1] Federal Decree No. 33 for the year 2000 concerning Judicial Co-operation between the UAE and India, F.G No. 346 dated 29 March 2000.

1. An official copy of the decree;
2. a certificate showing that the decree is final and executable;
3. in case of a decree *in absentia*, an authenticated copy of the summons or any other document showing that the defendant was duly summoned; and
4. if the request is only for execution of a decree, an official copy in properly executable form.

Chapter Four

COMMENCEMENT OF PROCEEDINGS

The Civil Procedure Law applies to each stage of the litigation process and the procedural requirements must be followed. Apart from minor differences between certain Emirates, the process usually follows the procedure set out in this chapter.

4.1 Initiating Action

4.1.1 Reconciliation Committees at the Federal Courts

It is now compulsory for the parties initiating an action in a Federal court to comply with Federal Law No. 4 of 2001[1] regarding the establishment of Reconciliation Committees at Federal courts in the UAE. This is not applicable in Dubai or Ras Al Khaimah.

This law was passed on the 3rd of January 2001 and provides for the appointment of one or more reconciliation committees at the Federal courts of First Instance by the Minister of Justice. The committees consist of two members of the Judicial Authority and are presided by a Judge.[2] The purpose of the reconciliation committees is to encourage and facilitate the amicable settlement of commercial and civil disputes of whatever value.

The reconciliation committees have access to all records, documents and evidence it may require and is located at the court itself. The Ministerial Decree No. 133 of 2001 regarding the Duties of Mediation and Conciliation Committees indicates that procedures pertaining to hearing the dispute must follow the stipulations of the Civil Procedure Law.[3]

---

[1] Federal Law No. 4 of 2001, amending Federal Law No. 26 of 1999, regarding the Establishment of Reconciliation Committees at Federal courts in the UAE.

[2] Article 1 of Federal Law No. 4 of 2001.

[3] Article 2 of Ministerial Decree No. 133 of 2001.

Any party is, however, entitled to apply for a letter of no-objection from the relevant reconciliation committee should they not wish to resolve their dispute amicably. The Court of First Instance may not hear a case unless the matter has been before the relevant reconciliation committee or a letter of no-objection from the relevant reconciliation committee has been filed.[1]

The time periods specified by law for the hearing of a case and periods of prescription cease from the date of filing a dispute before a reconciliation committee.[2]

In terms of Article 2 of Federal Law No. 4 of 2001, reconciliation committees do not have authority over the following:

1. Summary and provisional orders and claims, labour claims, state cases, rent claims which are to be decided by rent mediation committees or any other cases to be considered by any other reconciliation committee.
2. If a claimant has imposed an attachment on his opponent's assets or taken any summary measures.
3. Cases filed before the Federal courts as from the date of validity of Federal Law No. 26 of 1999 until the date of enforcement of the Federal Law No. 4 of 2001.
4. The Ministerial Decree provides that the reconciliation committee may not look into any dispute in which the attendance of the public prosecutor is required.[3]
5. It may not look into any dispute relating to family matters of any kind or financial disputes that may arise from family issues.[4]

A reconciliation committee may not look into any dispute unless the parties to it are present and have signed an acceptance that the committee will look into their case, a copy of this acceptance must be filed.[5]

An application to the reconciliation committee must contain the addresses of the parties, details of the dispute, the subject of the application, supporting arguments together with all supporting documents. It must contain the date of the application and the signature of the applicant or his advocate.[6] The claimant is not required to pay any court fees at this stage.

---

[1] Article 1(3)1 of Federal Law No. 4 of 2001.

[2] Article 1(3)3 of Federal Law No. 4 of 2001.

[3] Article 3 of Ministerial Decree No. 133 of 2001.

[4] Article 4 of Ministerial Decree No. 133 of 2001.

[5] Article 9 of Ministerial Decree No. 133 of 2001.

[6] Article 10 of Ministerial Decree No. 133 of 2001.

In the event that the parties are able to reach reconciliation, the reconciliation committee will submit such an agreement to the court where it will be made an order of court and may be executed as a judgment. If the parties are unable to reach reconciliation, the reconciliation committee will pass the matter on to the court. At this point, the claimant has the option to proceed or not. If he decides to proceed, the court fees must be paid and the case will proceed in the normal manner.

4.1.2 Statement of Claim

An action commences when the claimant or his advocate files a Statement of Claim with the court which has jurisdiction to hear the matter.[1] The Statement of Claim is a formal written document setting out the name, address and designation of the claimant and of the defendant, the facts (in brief) of the case and the remedy the claimant seeks from the court, together with supporting documents and certified Arabic translations thereof if needed.

The Statement of Claim varies in length depending on the complexity of the action, however, in practice, a Statement of Claim is approximately 3 - 5 pages long. The Statement of Claim must be drafted in Arabic as Arabic is the language of the courts[2] and it must be signed by the claimant or his representative. The claimant need not file original supporting documents, however, if the copy is challenged before the court he may be ordered to file the original to allow the copy to be compared to the original.[3]

The claimant must submit copies of the Statement of Claim and supporting documents sufficient for each defendant and one for the Clerk of the Court.[4] It must be noted that if the action is filed by an advocate on behalf of the claimant, an original Power of Attorney, duly notarized, must be filed with the Statement of Claim. If the Power of Attorney originated outside the UAE, it must be notarised, legalised and authenticated by the UAE Embassy and the Ministry of Foreign Affairs in the United Arab Emirates, before filing.[5]

---

[1] Article 42 of the Civil Procedure Law.

[2] Article 4 of the Civil Procedure Law.

[3] Article 9 of Federal Law No. 10 of 1992 (Law of Evidence).

[4] Article 45(1) of the Civil Procedure Law.

[5] Dubai Court of Cassation Judgment 264/92 dated 14 February 1993.

The Statement of Claim together with all supporting documents and the requisite copies must be filed with the Clerk of the Court. The claimant is required to pay court fees and once paid a voucher will be issued.[1] Court fees are usually calculated on the basis of the amount claimed and this fee may vary from one Emirate to another.[2]

Once the court fees have been paid, the documents are in order and the addresses of the claimant and the defendant are provided, the Clerk of the Court will open a file for the matter, allocate a case number and schedule a hearing date for the action. A hearing date will be scheduled within two weeks to one month from the date on which the Statement of Claim is filed. There are no hard and fast rules for this as it often depends on the availability of the Judge and the workload of the court.

The claimant will be informed of the date allocated and a summons will be prepared for service on the defendant.

In normal circumstances it takes approximately one hour to complete the formalities to file a suit before the UAE courts, including payment of the court fees. The Statement of Claim can only be filed during office hours which are from 7.30 am to 2.30 pm, however, payment of court fees may not be possible after 1.30 pm.

If the action involves a special dispensation such as exemption of the court fees,[3] scheduling a hearing for exceptional reasons or an unusual claim or remedy, or any other special or unusual circumstances, then the matter will be put to the Chief Justice of the court to adjudicate upon. This process may take a few hours before the file returns to the Clerk of the Court with the Chief Justice's recommendations or comments on the matter.

Neither the Chief Justice, nor the Clerk of the Court, will decide on any issue involving the substance of the claim or the nature of the action or the remedies sought. The Clerk of the Court will register the Statement of Claim even if the court concerned has no jurisdiction on the matter, as this is a matter for the Judge to decide once the matter is heard before the court.

---

[1] Supreme Court of Cassation Judgment 4 for the year 19 dated 8 October 1997, Dubai Court of Cassation Judgment 2/98 dated 10 January 1999.

[2] See Appendix 1.

[3] Article 6 of Federal Decree No. 15 for the year 1992 regarding court Fees before the Federal court, Dubai Court of Cassation Judgment 241/93 dated 12 February 1994.

4.1.3 The Summons

Once the Statement of Claim has been filed and a hearing date scheduled for the case, the Clerk of the Court will prepare the summons. The summons must include the following information:[1]

1. The day, month, year and hour of service;
2. The name, title, profession, domicile and place of work of the claimant and the defendant;
3. The name and details of the person undertaking the service;
4. The subject matter of the summons;
5. The name and title of the person to whom the summons has been delivered, and his signature or seal acknowledging receipt; and
6. The case number and the date of hearing of the case.

On the day following the day the Statement of Claim was filed, the Clerk of the Court shall hand the summons, with a copy of the Statement of Claim and the supporting documents attached, to the court bailiff for service on the defendant in the proceedings.[2]

4.2 Service

The summons will be served on each defendant at the address provided. It is advisable for the claimant or the claimant's representative to accompany the court bailiff to affect the service of the summons on the defendant. The summons must be served on the defendant on a working day, not before 07.00 am nor after 06.00 p.m.[3]

Service of the summons must be carried out on the defendant himself or his authorised agent or advocate. Service on an agent or an advocate will not be valid unless the claimant provides evidence that the person who has been served is the authorised agent of the defendant or holds a power of attorney for the defendant, thereby enabling such person to accept service on the defendant's behalf. Summons must be served within 10 days from the date the summons was handed to the court bailiff. In the event that the date of

---

[1] Article 7 of the Civil Procedure Law.

[2] Article 46 of the Civil Procedure Law. Dubai Court of Cassation Judgment 162/92 dated 13 December 1992, Dubai Court of Cassation Judgment 396/94 dated 26 February 1995, Supreme Court of Cassation Judgment 74 for the year 20 dated 28 September 1999, Supreme Court of Cassation Judgment 389 for the year 21 dated 28 February 2001.

[3] Article 6 of the Civil Procedure Law.

the hearing falls within this period, service must be affected before the hearing date.[1]

In general, the service of summons may go through one of the following procedures:

4.2.1 Local Service

If the defendant resides within the Emirate in which the action was filed, the summons will be served on the defendant in person at his domicile or place of work.[2] The summons must be served on the defendant or his duly authorised representative. Service can be affected on a person living with the defendant who is 18 years old or over who does not have a conflict of interest.[3]

In the case of a legal entity such as a company, association or establishment, summons must be served at the head office of the concern to the officer in charge (such as the owner, general manager or partner, if the concern is a partnership). If no officer is present, a copy of the summons may be left with a member of staff at the office.[4] If the concern has no head office a copy should be delivered to the person who represents the concern either personally or at his place of domicile.[5]

However, if the summons is served on an employee or person living with the defendant, the summons will need to be served a second time, as more fully dealt with below.

Although the service of summons is the responsibility of the court, the court considers following up the service of summons and ensuring that the address of the defendant is correct as the responsibility of the claimant.[6] The claimant should confirm that service has taken place prior to the hearing date and must ensure that the summons has been properly served on the right party to the action at the right address.

---

[1] Article 46 of the Civil Procedure Law.

[2] Article 8 of the Civil Procedure Law.

[3] Article 8(3) of the Civil Procedure Law.

[4] Article 9(2) of the Civil Procedure Law.

[5] Article 9(2) of the Civil Procedure Law.

[6] Dubai Court of Cassation Judgment 319/98 dated 9 January 1999.

4.2.2 Service in Another Emirate

The service of notices upon defendants from one Emirate to another must be effected in accordance with Articles 5, 6 and 7 of Federal Law No. 11 of 1973[1], which law governs the judicial relationship between the individual Emirates of the UAE. These articles govern the procedure of petition or deputation of a court in one Emirate to a court in another Emirate for the implementation of a judgment or service of summons or enforcement of any order which needs to be enforced in another Emirate. Service of summons directly to a person in another Emirate without going through the correct procedure, is not proper service.

The Civil Procedure Law also contains provisions for deputation, service of summons and enforcement of decisions from one court to another. It is not be possible to execute judgments or effect service of summons in another Emirate, except through a deputation from one Emirate to another. Therefore, if the action is filed in one Emirate and the defendant is domiciled or has his place of business in another Emirate, a petition must be made to the court of the other Emirate to effect the service of summons.

For example, if the Dubai court needs to serve a summons on a person domiciled in Sharjah, then the summons must be sent to Sharjah court and that court bailiff of that court will effect the service of the summons on the defendant. The bailiff of the Sharjah court will return the summons to the Dubai court confirming service on the defendant or any other comments that the court bailiff may have in connection therewith. It is advisable for the claimant or the claimant's representative to monitor this process throughout to ensure that the summons has been forwarded to the other court, that service has been effected and confirmation to this effect has been returned to the court concerned, prior to the first hearing.

If service is to be executed from one Emirate to another, the party should allow approximately 10 days to two weeks for service to be effected and for notice of the service to be returned to the court. The Civil Procedure Law allows for an additional ten days for service upon a person in another Emirate.[2]

---

[1] Regulating the Judicial Relationship between the Emirates.

[2] Article 12(1) of the Civil Procedure Law.

4.2.3   Service of Summons in a Foreign Jurisdiction

If it is clear from the Statement of Claim that the defendant is domiciled outside the UAE, the Clerk of the Court will ask the claimant to have the summons, the Statement of Claim and all supporting documents translated into English. Once this is done, the documents will be forwarded to the Federal Ministry of Justice to effect service on the defendant abroad. The Ministry of Justice in turn will forward the summons and attachments to the Ministry of Foreign Affairs who will then forward the documents to the UAE Embassy in the country where the defendant is domiciled, to effect service on the defendant in that jurisdiction.

The Civil Procedure Law allows for an additional 60 days for service upon a person who is domiciled outside of the UAE.[1] The Clerk of the Court, in such a case, will schedule a hearing for the case at least 3 months in advance, to allow for the summons to be returned. Once the summons is served on the defendant in the place where he is domiciled, the Ministry of Justice will forward evidence to the Clerk of the Court that the summons has been properly served via political channels. This will then be considered valid service to enable the courts to proceed with the action.

In practice, however, effecting service through political channels takes a long time and on occasion, proof of service is not returned within the period of three months. In such a case the matter will be adjourned for a further 3 months to allow for the service to be properly effected, or to allow for proof of service to be received. The UAE courts do not recognise service of summons by fax, courier service or through the claimant directly. Foreign service can only be effected through diplomatic channels as provided by the law.[2]

4.2.4   Alternative Methods of Service

The case will not proceed until the proof of service is received and the court will not accept an alternative method for service unless it has become apparent that the defendant is no longer domiciled at the address provided by the claimant. The summons must be returned with confirmation that it has or it has not been served, for any reason, for the court to consider an alternative method of service.

---

[1] Article 12(1) of the Civil Procedure Law.

[2] See for example the provisions of the G.C.C Treaty.

Service by Publication

In the event that:

1. the claimant does not know the address or location of the defendant; or
2. should the claimant prove that the defendant has moved location and he is unable to locate the defendants presence anywhere in the UAE or abroad; or
3. in the event that the service of summons whether carried out locally or in another Emirate or abroad returns with the remark from the court bailiff that he was unable to locate the defendant at the address shown; or
4. that the defendant has closed down; or
5. moved premises and the court bailiff has no knowledge of his whereabouts,

then the claimant may, at the hearing, ask the court to make an order allowing for the attachment of a copy of the summons to the door of the defendant's place of residence, or last known place of residence, or by publishing it in a widely circulated Arabic daily newspaper.[1] The claimant must show that he made every effort to locate the address of the defendant but that no address was found.[2]

The court, after considering the matter and assessing whether the claimant has made every effort to locate the defendant, may grant the claimant's request. In practice, if the defendant is an Arab national, publication must be carried out in an Arabic newspaper and if the defendant is a foreigner, publication must be carried out in both Arabic and an English newspaper. The date of publication shall be deemed to be the date of service of summons.[3]

If the court grants the right of publication, the publication must indicate the case number, the name of the claimant and the defendant, the amount claimed and the scheduled date of hearing. It should invite the defendant to attend the hearing, and indicate that should the defendant fail to attend, judgment will be delivered in absentia. The court will consider such a publication to be valid alternative service on the defendant to enable the court to proceed with the matter.

---

[1] Article 8(4) of the Civil Procedure Law.

[2] Dubai Court of Cassation Judgment 319/98 dated 9 January 1999, Dubai Court of Cassation Judgment 115/2002 dated 18 May 2002, Dubai Court of Cassation judgment 172/2002 dated 29 June 2002.

[3] Dubai Court of Cassation Judgment 374/98 dated 19 December 1998.

The court usually grants service by publication only in extraordinary circumstances.[1] An order for publication can only be granted by the court at the hearing of the case and not by the Clerk of the Court.

Service by Announcement on the Court Board

In the event that:

1. the defendant refuses to accept service of the summons; or
2. the business has closed and the court bailiff is unable to enter the premises to serve the summons; or
3. if one of the household members is present but the defendant refuses to come forward to receive the summons,

then in terms of the Civil Procedure Law, the court bailiff must immediately report this matter to the Judge for a decision to effect the service in a manner which the Judge deems fit.[2] The Judge may order service by the same means or order the court bailiff to attach the summons to the door of the defendant's address as provided.[3] In this event the court bailiff will also attach a copy of the summons on the court's board. This will be considered a 'proper' service on the defendant under such circumstances.[4]

4.2.5 Service to be Effected Twice

In terms of the Civil Procedure Law, if the defendant fails to attend the first hearing of the matter, in spite of the fact that service was properly effected by one of the procedures outlined above, the court may decide to effect service on him a second time before proceeding with the matter.[5]

This will not be the case if service is effected upon a defendant in person, but will apply if not served personally or if the authorized representative (usually the general manager) of a company is not served personally. In such cases service must be affected a second time and at this stage service will be valid even if served upon a family member or employee. If the

---

[1] Supreme Court of Cassation Judgment 268 for the year 18 dated 29 October 1996, Dubai Court of Cassation Judgment 22/98 dated 4 November 1998, Dubai Court of Cassation Judgment 23/2001 dated 1 April 2001.

[2] Article 5(2) of the Civil Procedure Law.

[3] Article 8(4) of the Civil Procedure Law.

[4] Dubai Court of Cassation Judgment 391/ 99 dated 13 February 2000.

[5] Article 53 of the Civil Procedure Law. Dubai Court of Cassation Judgment 132/97 dated 19 July 1997.

defendant fails to attend after service has been affected the second time, the court will proceed with the action and will consider the service to be valid.

Summary of Technical Requirements for Valid Service

In order for service of summons to be valid, the following criteria must be followed:

1. The summons may not be served before 7.00am or after 6.00pm nor on public holidays, except in an emergency and upon written authorization by a Judge of summary matters. As to the government or public legal persons, service shall only be effected during working hours.[1]

2. The summons itself must contain the information referred to in Article 7.

3. The summons must be served on the defendant at his place of work or his domicile. If the defendant is not found at his domicile, it may be delivered to any person living with him. If the defendant is not found at his place of work, it may be delivered to a person who can confirm that he is responsible for the administration at the defendant's place of work. In both cases the recipient of the summons must be more than 18 years of age and may not have an interest in conflict with that of the defendant. If there are no such persons available, or such persons are not qualified to accept service, then the bailiff must notify the Judge in order that he may make an order for alternative service. In such a case the Judge may order that the summons be fixed to the door of the defendant's domicile, or place of work and a copy be placed on the court notice board, or that the summons be published in a widely circulated Arabic daily newspaper.[2]

4. The summons must be served within the prescribed time periods[3], these time periods are increased if the parties reside in another jurisdiction or outside the country.[4]

5. If the summons is not served upon the defendant or its authorized representative personally, it must be served twice, this is applicable at each level of the court, i.e. the Court of First Instance, Appeal and Cassation.

6. The claimant accordingly has a duty to carry out a proper investigation of the defendant's address before commencing the action.

7. Invalid service will annul the judgment at any stage and can be raised at any stage.

---

[1] Article 6 of the Civil Procedure Law.

[2] Article 8 of the Civil Procedure Law.

[3] Article 11 of the Civil Procedure Law.

[4] Article 12 of the Civil Procedure Law.

4.2.6   Challenging the Service of Summons

Challenging the service of a summons or the address provided by the claimant can only be done in court. However, such a challenge serves no real legal purpose as the court will consider the fact that the defendant or his representative appeared before the court in order to challenge the service as evidence that the service must have been valid. The court will also usually allow an invalid procedure to be rectified.[1] Therefore, there are no legal benefits of challenging service of summons if the case has not yet been reserved for judgment at the Court of First Instance. An application or appeal against improper service may be filed at any stage, even after final judgment.

If the judgment is delivered and the service effected is considered to be invalid, the defendants may challenge the judgment on the grounds that the service of the summons was improper. This can be done by submitting an application to the same court or by appealing to the Court of Appeal. On consideration of the application, if the court decides that the service of summons was not valid then the appeal period does not lapse and the defendant can appeal against the decision. If the court finds that the service was not a "proper" service then the judgment will be set aside and it will be considered to be null and void. The matter will be referred back to the Court of First Instance or in other cases the claimant may be required to re-institute all the proceedings.[2]

4.3   Proceeding with the Main Action

Once service has been effected the court will proceed with the case in the normal manner unless it is an urgent matter or is an application for an attachment.

4.3.1   The Defendant's Response

In terms of the Civil Procedure Law, the defendant is required to file his response (defence) at least three days before the first hearing of the case.[3] However, in practice, it is usual for the defendant to attend the court at the

---

[1] Article 15 of the Civil Procedure Law.

[2] Dubai Court of Cassation Judgment 329/2000 dated 16 December 2000, Dubai Court of Cassation Judgment 336/2000 dated 14 January 2001.

[3] Article 45(2) of the Civil Procedure Law.

first hearing to request an adjournment to respond to the action[1] and such an adjournment will usually be granted. The defendant will be required to file his response (together with supporting documents) to the action filed by the claimant at the following hearing. In his response, the defendant may either make an admission to the allegations contained in the claimant's Statement of Claim, deny them and set out his defence. The defendant may at the same time submit a counterclaim.[2]

The claimant will normally require time to comment on the submissions made by the defendant. The case is therefore likely to go back and forth between the claimant and the defendant with the exchange of memoranda and documents.

If, after the third or fourth hearing the only submissions made are the memoranda, the court may reserve the case for judgment even if the claimant or the defendant require more time to comment. However, if documentation is submitted, in almost every case the court will grant an extension to whichever party requests it to allow them time to comment on the submission.[3] Documents and pleadings are in practice only exchanged at hearings and therefore the court will always grant whoever requests the right, time to comment on the documents submitted at the hearing.

4.3.2 Preliminary Defences

The defendant may attempt to have the case dismissed before trial through various pre-trial motions. For instance, the defendant may submit to the court arguments:

1. challenging the jurisdiction of the court; or
2. in order to stay the proceedings by raising lack of jurisdiction; or
3. the title of the claimant to sue; or
4. any other preliminary arguments which the defendant would like the court to decide upon including the right to stay proceedings on the grounds that the parties have agreed to refer their disputes to arbitration.

In the UAE, however, the courts are often reluctant to decide on the preliminary arguments of the case. Instead, the courts often ask the parties to submit their preliminary arguments together with their submissions on the merits of the case. Following due consideration of the submissions, the

---

[1] Article 73(1) of the Civil Procedure Law.

[2] Article 99 of the Civil Procedure law.

[3] Article 70 of the Civil Procedure Law.

court may either reserve the case for judgment and decide upon it or dismiss the case based on the preliminary arguments.

Only rarely and at its sole discretion, does the court make a judgment based on the preliminary defences without dealing with the merits. The court may, however, once the case is reserved for judgment, grant the party his remedy or make an order based on the preliminary defences.[1]

4.4 Counterclaim

If the Defendant has a cause of action against the claimant, this may be raised either by separate proceedings or by way of a counterclaim in the existing action. This is known as the defence and counterclaim. There are no special requirements for filing a counterclaim other than that it must be submitted orally at the hearing or by application to court.[2] The court will admit a counterclaim for an action subject to the following conditions:

1. The counterclaim must be filed at an early stage of the proceedings and only in the Court of First Instance prior to reservation of judgment. Although there is no time limit for filing, it is however established that it should be filed in the early stages of the case and not when the case reserved for judgment. If filed just prior to the reservation of judgment, this may be construed as a delaying tactic on the part of the defendants and the court may reject the application.
2. Following the filing of the counterclaim, the court fees must be paid to the Clerk of the Court. If the court fees have not been paid a counterclaim will not be heard.
3. The counterclaim must relate to the same subject matter. It is not necessary to have resulted from the same cause of action in the main action.
4. The counterclaim is filed against an existing party to the main action, whether that is the claimant or defendant in the main action.
5. The counterclaim could be filed in a separate Statement of Claim or in the same response, however, it must be clear that the defendant intends to file a counterclaim and is seeking a remedy and is not simply responding to the action.

---

[1] Supreme Court of Cassation Judgment 81 for the year 17 dated 31 March 1996.

[2] Supreme Court of Cassation Judgment 164 for the year 15 dated 15 February 1994, Supreme Court of Cassation Judgment 360 and 240 for the year 19 dated 1 December 1998.

While it is at the discretion of the court whether to admit a counterclaim, the court will normally do so, unless the counterclaim is filed at a late stage of the proceedings. The court will hear the counterclaim and when the case is reserved for judgment the court will decide whether to accept the counterclaim, adjudicate on it, or dismiss it on its merits.[1]

Ultimately, judgment will be delivered in the main action and the counterclaim and each judgment shall bear an individual court reference number. Either party to the action may appeal against the judgment in respect of the main action and the counterclaim to the Court of Appeal.

As mentioned, the defendant in an action is not required to file his counterclaim in the main action. He may file his counterclaim in a separate proceeding before the court.

If the counterclaim is filed separately it will be treated as a separate action and may be heard by a different court. However, the court may, upon the request of the claimant in the main action and provided that both actions are related to the same matter, join the two actions. This is assuming that the counterclaim has been filed with the same court in the same jurisdiction as the main action. It is not possible to join two actions filed in two separate courts in two different Emirates.

Upon application by either party, it may be possible for one of the actions to be suspended pending a decision by the other court in the action in order to avoid contradictions in the two judgments. This is at the discretion of the courts involved, although it is likely if the decision of one court may adversely affect the outcome of the other action.

The court may, at its discretion, accept the filing of a counterclaim even if the court has decided to refer the matter to an expert or following the submission of the expert's report or after the court has heard the testimony of the witnesses.[2]

---

[1] Dubai Court of Cassation Judgment 85/94 dated 16 October 1994.

[2] Supreme Court of Cassation Judgment 247 for the year 15 dated 19 June 1994, Dubai Court of Cassation Judgment 262/96 dated 1 February 1997, Dubai Court of Cassation Judgment no 218/96 dated 11 May 1997, Dubai Court of Cassation Judgment 165/97 dated 5 July 1997, Dubai Court of Cassation Judgment 18/97 dated 26 October 1997, Dubai Court of Cassation Judgment 257/98 dated 14 November 1998, Dubai Court of Cassation Judgment 148/99 dated 6 June 1999.

4.5 Interlocutory Applications

Any application made, be it an application for a preliminary attachment, joinder, an application to refer the matter for forensic testing (forgery) or an application to refer the matter to an expert, may be made at any stage verbally or in writing. The Judge in turn may decide to deal with the application or to leave it until the matter is reserved for judgment.[1]

4.6 Witnesses

In the UAE, being a civil law jurisdiction, there will not be a lengthy trial involving the testimony of many witnesses. Normally, all arguments, comments and documents submitted to the court are made by way of written submissions. However, upon the request of either party, and if the value of the claim exceeds AED 5,000,[2] witnesses may be called. The request must be made by the party concerned, the Judge will not call witnesses of his own accord.[3]

In addition, even if the value of the claim exceeds AED 5,000 witnesses may not be called if the witnesses' testimony contradicts written evidence, if the liability can only be proved in writing or if, by a later amendment, the amount is reduced to less than AED 5,000.[4]

If the court agrees to allow the calling of witnesses it will postpone the matter to allow the party who has requested witnesses, time to call those witnesses. If the court so decides it will also give the other party the right to call counter witnesses before the court.[5] In such a case the court will schedule a hearing for both parties to bring their witnesses. They all may be heard at one hearing or the case may be adjourned for two or three hearings to allow the witnesses to be heard.

The witnesses will be questioned first by the party who has called them and then cross-examined by the other party. The court also has the right to question the witnesses to clarify certain points during the questioning or the

---

[1] Supreme Court of Cassation Judgment 30 and 41 for the year 20 dated 13 June 2000, Dubai Court of Cassation Judgment 397/2000 and 411/2000 dated 4 February 2001.

[2] Article 35 of the Law of Evidence.

[3] Dubai Court of Cassation Judgment 216/98 dated 12 December 1998, Dubai Court of Cassation Judgment 16/2000 dated 28 May 2000.

[4] Article 36 of the Law of Evidence.

[5] Article 39 of the Law of Evidence.

cross-examination.[1] The court will then hear the other party's witnesses at the same hearing or at a subsequent hearing and the other party will also be given the right to cross-examination.

Either party may bring witnesses irrespective of nationality, religion, language or gender. There are no restrictions on the number of witnesses although the courts are usually not willing to hear more than three witnesses per party except in exceptional circumstances.[2]

The following witnesses cannot be heard before the court and their statements will not be accepted before the court:

1. Brothers or sisters unless they are heard in criminal proceedings.
2. A person who has an interest in the matter or that of who may benefit or refute a claim against him.
3. A lawyer who is involved in the case because of confidentiality as it is prohibited under the UAE Advocacy law.
4. A Judge or a clerk who has been involved in the case at any stage.
5. A person who has been charged and found guilty of a crime which indicates that he is dishonest and has committed a felony.

It has, however been held by the UAE court that if a party wishes to challenge the other party's witnesses, then this matter must be brought before the court prior to putting the witness on the stand to testify. If a party fails to challenge the necessity of a witness he will be considered to have waived his rights to do so at a later stage. This rule is applied except where a matter of public policy is involved, in which case the court may permit a challenge to be brought at any time.

Witnesses will be required to swear an oath and provide the court with an identity document declaring their name, addresses and age before they will be accepted to testify. The Clerk of the Court will note all questions and answers down. If the witness does not speak Arabic the court will provide with a translator for him. It is advisable to make prior arrangements in this regard with the Clerk of the Court to ensure that a translator is available and not engaged in another court.

---

[1] Article 44 of the Law of Evidence.

[2] Supreme Court of Cassation Judgment 314 for the year 18 dated 26 November 1996, Dubai Court of Cassation Judgment 93/97 dated 19 October 1997, Dubai Court of Cassation Judgment 252/97 dated 21 December 1997, Dubai Court of Cassation Judgment 16/2000 dated 28 May 2000, Dubai Court of Cassation Judgment 388/2000 dated 4 February 2001, Dubai Court of Cassation Judgment 5/2001 dated 1 April 2001.

4.7 Expert Witnesses[1]

Either party may, during their submissions and before the case is reserved for judgment ask the court to refer the matter to an expert. The term 'expert' in this context means a person specialised in dealing with the specific or technical facts of the case, such as an auditor, a marine expert, or an engineering expert. The purpose of the expert is to assist the court in understanding the facts of the case and the technical arguments made by either party.

Once the case is reserved for judgment, the court may decide, either at its own discretion or at the request of either party, to call upon an expert to look into the technical aspects of the case. There is no provision for an appeal against the order, however a party may appeal against the identity of the expert. An appeal against the identity of the expert must be filed within three days, although the identity of an expert may be challenged within a week of the appointment.[2]

The court will then assign a mandate to the expert which he needs to comply with to complete his work. The court often asks the expert to review the documents and the submissions made by the parties, meet both parties and discuss the case with them, investigate the matter at any government department or within the private sector that the expert deems necessary, hear the witnesses of both parties and any other person relevant to the case before submitting his report to the court.

The procedure for the selection of experts in the Federal court is that the court will approach the Ministry of Justice to recommend an expert from the list of experts employed by the Ministry of Justice. If there is no expert available with specific expertise in a particular matter, an external expert or academic will be appointed. The list of experts previously maintained by the Ministry of Justice is now used only for the appointment of custodians or liquidators.

The procedure has also changed in Dubai and experts in financial, auditing or commercial matters are now often appointed from the auditors employed by the Government of Dubai (internal auditors) based at the Ruler's Court. However, the previous list of experts may still be referred to, or an academic appointed or an expert as agreed by the parties.

---

[1] Articles 69-92 of the Law of Evidence.

[2] Article 78 of the Law of Evidence.

The court will also order one or both parties to pay the fees of the expert. The case will then be adjourned until the expert files his report.

4.7.1 Duties of the Expert

The expert will normally invite both parties to meet at his office for a meeting or several meetings to investigate the matter according to the mandate provided by the court. He will also invite the parties to submit to him documents, arguments, suggestions and witnesses or suggestions in order to investigate the matter before reaching his findings. This may go on for months and may involve several meetings jointly or separately.

Once the expert finalises his report he will file it in court with a copy to both parties. Both parties will then be given the opportunity to comment on the report and to submit further evidence before the case is reserved for judgment. On occasion, the court may reserve the case for judgment and refer the matter back to the expert to deal with arguments or challenges that are raised by the parties or the Judge to clarify further any issue that the court believes needs clarification or calls for expertise.

An "outside" expert, upon filing his report or the supplementary reports may ask the court to pay him an additional fee or to assess his work and grant him fee additional to the amount already paid through the courts.

An expert's opinion is considered valuable in the UAE and usually the more complicated or technical cases are referred to an expert. There may be more than one expert appointed. The courts often rely heavily on the expert's report and opinions when adjudicating the case, although this is entirely at the discretion of the court. The court may take into consideration the expert's report or opinions in whole or in part or discount it altogether. The court also has the power to refer the matter to another expert on the same issues that were assigned to the previous expert or to deal with an additional assignment, which the court needs to clarify before adjudicating the case.

4.8 Documents

In the UAE, photocopies of documents are normally accepted in court, whether the documents originated in or out of the UAE.[1] Either party to the action may, however, challenge any document filed in court, in which case the original must be produced,[2] failing which the document in question may be set aside by the Judge and not taken into consideration. The court will always accept official (government) documentation as evidence and such documentation may not be challenged.

If there is sufficient evidence which substantiates the facts evidenced in a copy of a document, the court is often of the opinion that challenging the documents to file the original is only a delaying tactic.

If the documents are alleged to have been issued by one of the parties in the proceedings and that party denies the signature on the document,[3] then it may be referred by the court to an expert to verify the signature or it may be set aside provided that:[4]

1. That the party involved does not dispute the document or the contents of it before denying the signature.
2. That there is no other evidence or fact in the case which substantiates the fact that the document has been issued by the party in connection with the transactions i.e. there is another reference to this document in the correspondence submitted to the court.
3. That the party has initiated criminal action for forgery in respect of the document under investigation.

If a criminal action is filed by a party based on a document filed in court with an alleged forged signature, and depending upon the value of that document to the case, the court may suspend civil proceedings subject to the outcome of the criminal proceedings. Following the filing of evidence before the civil Judge that a criminal action has been initiated, the Judge in the civil court may suspend the civil action pending the outcome of the criminal investigation. The Judge may, also, at his own discretion, refer the

---

[1] Article 13 of the Law of Evidence. Dubai Court of Cassation Judgment 455/98 dated 30 January 1999.

[2] Supreme Court of Cassation Judgment 629 for the year 18 dated 29 November 1998.

[3] Article 11 of the Law of Evidence.

[4] Dubai Court of Cassation Judgment 75/96 dated 11 January 1997.

document to a CID laboratory for testing to verify the signature and the document.[1]

The court, however, acknowledges that communications and commercial transactions can be carried out in a fast and speedy manner and without formalities and therefore fax copies of documents and carbon copies of documents will be admissible in court.[2]

Regarding electronic communications such as email, there is no Federal information technology legislation at present although a draft is currently being reviewed by a special committee established by the Ministry of Justice and Islamic affairs for this purpose. It is understood that this law will consist of articles dealing with digital signatures and issues relating to signing and forgery of electronic documents. There is furthermore nothing concerning electronic documents or electronic signatures in the Federal Law of Evidence as yet.

In Dubai, however, the following laws have been issued:

<u>Dubai Law concerning the Use of Computers in Criminal Procedures</u>[3]

Pursuant to this law, documents with electronic signatures will be admissible as evidence in criminal investigations. The provisions of this law acknowledge signatures of individuals acquired through the use of computers and other means of information technology for the purposes of proof in criminal cases. The record of the investigation at the Prosecutor's Office may be entirely electronic and submitted to the court in electronic form. A smart card identifying the user by fingerprints is utilized to enter a document. Regulations to this law have been published and set out the procedures for enforcing the articles of this law.

---

[1] Supreme Court of Cassation Judgment 110 for the year 13 dated 14 April 1993, Dubai Court of Cassation Judgment 47/2000 and 95 /2000 dated 4 June 2000, Dubai Court of Cassation Judgment 24/2001 dated 5 May 2001.

[2] Dubai Court of Cassation Judgment 160/95 dated 9 December 1995, Dubai Court of Cassation Judgment 31/96 dated 26 October 1996, Dubai Court of Cassation Judgment 118/98 dated 20 June 1998, Dubai Court of Cassation Judgment 66/2000 dated 20 May 2000.

[3] Dubai Law No. 5 of 2001 concerning the Use of Computers in Criminal Procedures.

Dubai Electronic Transactions and Commerce Law[1]

Amongst other things, this law deals with electronic messages, electronic registers and electronic signatures in terms of which electronic messages shall not be denied legal effect, validity or enforceability solely on the ground that it is in electronic format. Provided that the requirements of access and storage set out in the law are satisfied, an electronic document or file shall be regarded as equivalent to a written document required by any law. Further, the Law has recognised electronic signatures and outlined the criteria according to which an electronic signature shall be regarded as equivalent to a handwritten signature. In addition, electronic information shall have evidential value and its evidential value shall be assessed in accordance with certain considerations set out in the Law.[2]

This Law has yet to be tested in the Dubai courts. Certain other laws dealing with electronic commerce are under consideration on a Federal and local level.

4.9 Discovery

Discovery refers to the rights of opposing parties to obtain information from each other prior to trial. There is no system of discovery under the UAE Civil Procedure Law. While discovery plays an important part of trials in the common law system and most popular in the US legal system, it is not recognised in the UAE. Under the Law of Evidence, however, either party may ask permission from the Judge to see or to receive a copy of any document submitted by the other party or mentioned as relevant in supporting their case.[3] The Judge may then order the other party to make the document available, provided that:

1. There is sufficient evidence to show the Judge that the document is in the possession of the other party and that they are able to produce or exhibit the same.
2. The other party has relied on that document in the court proceedings or referred to it in their pleadings but have not exhibited the same to the courts.

---

[1] Dubai Electronic Transactions and Commerce Law No. 2 of 2002 dated 12 February 2002.

[2] Article 12 of the Dubai Electronic Transactions and Commerce Law No. 2 of 2002.

[3] Article 18 of the Law of Evidence.

If the other party is ordered to produce the document they must make available the same unless they are able to convince the Judge to a reasonable extent that such documents are not in their possession or that there is a practical difficulty for them to access the document in question.

Furthermore, the UAE Commercial Code[1] provides that the books of a merchant may be used as evidence for or against him. Merchants in the UAE are not compelled to disclose information nor required to maintain proper books of account. Although they should maintain books of account, there are no ramifications if they do not do so, and it will not prove anything against the merchant. However, if the merchant does keep proper books of account and they are in a proper order, it may be to his advantage.[2]

4.10 Joinder

Following the filing of an action, even after the case has reached the court, the claimant may ask the court to join another defendant to the action.[3] This may be in partnership with the first defendant or as an independent defendant to the action. Generally, the claimant is entitled to join another defendant in the action if there is "just cause" why he had failed to join him at the commencement of the proceedings.[4]

The claimant must provide evidence that the joinder of the defendant relates to the claimant's cause of action against the defendant and in respect of the same subject matter. If the court is of the opinion that the joinder is relevant to the subject matter of the action, and that there are no particular legal grounds for not joining him in the action, the court will grant the claimant the right to sue the new defendant. The case will then be adjourned to enable the claimant to serve summons on the defendant and the service will follow the procedures outlined above.[5]

---

[1] Articles 36 and 37 of Federal Law No. 18 of 1993.

[2] Dubai Court of Cassation Judgment 427/97 dated 2 May 1998, Dubai Court of Cassation Judgment 457/98 dated 14 March 1999, Dubai Court of Cassation Judgment 253/2000 dated 12 November 2000.

[3] Article 94 of the Civil Procedure Law.

[4] Supreme Court of Cassation Judgment 332 for the year 16 dated 21 March 1995, Dubai Court of Cassation Judgment 478/98 dated 13 March 1999, Dubai Court of Cassation Judgment 46/2000 dated 20 May 2000.

[5] Supreme Court of Cassation Judgment 8 for the year 19 dated 3 May 1997, Dubai Court of Cassation Judgment 43/98 dated 2 May 1998.

Joining the new defendant does not require payment of any additional court fees. However, if the court is of the opinion that the case against the new defendant relates to a new cause of action, then the court may order the claimant to pay an additional fee for joining a new defendant to the action.

It is possible for one of the defendants to ask the court to join another defendant to the action. For example, in a case where the defendant has an insurance company covering his liability, the insurance company or any other party who were jointly responsible for the action would be joined as co-defendants in the proceedings with the defendant.[1] In such a case no court fees will be payable. However, if the defendant seeks an indemnity against the co-defendants should the first defendant be found liable, the courts may order the defendants to pay court fees. This is on the grounds that this request for an indemnity is a separate action.

It is also possible, and provided there are legal grounds to do so, for a person who has not been a party to the action, to ask the court to be joined as a claimant or defendant.[2] This may arise if another claimant is entitled to a remedy jointly with the original claimant. Similarly, the decision in a case may effect the legal position or the financial position of a party who is related to the subject matter of the proceedings. In such a case, the party may ask the court to join them in the proceedings as a claimant or defendant, as the case may be. The court, after careful consideration of the party's right to join in the action, will order the party to pay the proper court fees. The court will grant such an application only in limited circumstances where there is an immediate requirement to do so.[3]

A party may also apply to join a party to an action to compel them to produce certain documents which may be useful to the applicant in order to adduce certain evidence, even if the party so joined is not party to the cause of action, in other words, the only remedy sought against them is to compel them to file documents or provide information in their possession.[4]

---

[1] Dubai Court of Cassation Judgment 173/98 dated 31 October 1998, Dubai Court of Cassation Judgment 478/98 dated 13 March 1999.

[2] Article 95 of the Civil Procedure Law. Dubai Court of Cassation Judgment 140/97 dated 20 December 1997, Dubai Court of Cassation Judgment 51/2001 dated 30 December 2001.

[3] Dubai Court of Cassation Judgment 236/97 dated 18 October 1997.

[4] Dubai Court of Cassation Judgment 132/98 dated 21 November 1998.

The court itself, may of its own accord order the joinder of any person whom it considers should be included in the interests of justice or in order to reveal the truth.[1]

All the above applications must be made to the Court of First Instance before final judgment has been handed down.

It is not permissible for persons who were not litigants in a case to be joined in a matter before the Court of Appeal, unless the following conditions apply:[2]

1. A person requesting to be joined to one of the adversaries;
2. A person who is adversely affected by the appealed judgment (i.e. it is deemed to be proof against him.)

This is regarded as an exceptional procedure and will only be applied under limited circumstances.

4.11 Actions filed by or against Minors

Where it becomes evident to the court that one of the parties to the action is a minor, irrespective of whether he is represented by a guardian or not, the court must inform the prosecutor's office of the action and obtain their comments on the matter before proceeding further with the case.[3] The prosecutor's office will not be requested to join the action or to take any stand as a claimant or defendant, nor will they be requested to defend any of the parties including the minor.[4] The prosecutor's office may, however, file a memorandum or join the proceedings to protect the interests of the minor. If the court fails to notify the prosecutor's office, the judgment delivered against the minor may be null and void.[5]

Minors cannot pursue an action unless they are represented by a guardian. In the event of a dispute with a guardian, the Attorney General represented by the prosecutor's office will represent the minor.

---

[1] Article 96 of the Civil Procedure Law.

[2] Article 165(4) of the Civil Procedure Law. Dubai Court of Cassation Judgment 58/97 dated 11 October 1997.

[3] Dubai Court of Cassation Judgment 56/2000 dated 26 November 2000.

[4] Dubai Court of Cassation Judgment 51/2001 dated 30 December 2001.

[5] Dubai Court of Cassation Judgment 50/99 dated 30 May 1999.

Chapter Five

JUDGMENTS

5.1 Judgment

Once the parties have exchanged pleadings and submissions and the procedures relating to the trial have been concluded, the court will reserve the case for judgment, and a hearing date for the delivery thereof will be scheduled.[1] A judgment is the court's decision on the matter and the proceedings described above may take between one or two years before the case is reserved for judgment, especially if an expert has been appointed. Once a case is reserved for judgment, judgment will be rendered within two weeks to a month. In some instances, the court, on the date on which the judgment is scheduled to be delivered, may adjourn the case further for judgment, but may only do so once for the same reason.[2]

Judgment will be delivered in open court in the presence of both parties. The attendance of the claimant or the defendant is not compulsory nor will this have any effect on the judgment delivered. If a party fails to attend, judgment will be delivered *in absentia* provided that the parties were properly served in the first place. The only effect an *in absentia* judgment will have is on the timing of any future appeal which is more fully dealt with below.

The judgment will consist of a summary of the facts and arguments made together with an order or remedy granted by the court. A judgment is usually delivered unanimously, although a judgment delivered by a majority vote is valid.[3] The Judge will not give any reasons for the judgment on the day that the judgment is announced. The full text of the judgment will then

---

[1] Article 127 of the Civil Procedure Law.

[2] Article 127(1) of the Civil Procedure Law. Dubai Court of Cassation Judgment 341/98 dated 10 January 1999.

[3] Article 128(2) of the Civil Procedure Law.

be typed, signed by the Judge or the three Judges as the case may be and delivered to both parties within three days for summary judgments and ten days in other cases.[1] The judgment must contain the following information:[2]

1. The court which issues the judgment, the date and place of its issue, the type of case, the names of the Judges who heard the arguments, participated in the ruling and attended its pronouncement, the member of the public prosecution who expressed his opinion in the case, if any, the names of the litigants, their titles, capacities, domicile, place of work and their attendance or absence.
2. A summary of the facts of the case, the requests of the parties, a summary of the defence and the public prosecutor's opinion. The grounds for the judgment must be stated and the ruling.
3. The ruling must be signed by the President of the Session.[3]

5.2 Default Judgment

In terms of the Civil Procedure Law, if a defendant or his representative fails to appear before the Court of First Instance after being been properly summoned to do so on one or two occasions, (according to the procedure outlined above), default judgment will be granted.[4] If default judgment is delivered, a defendant will have no right to file for a review of the judgment or reopening of the case at any time, since a default judgment does not fall within one of the circumstances relating to a petition for a review.[5]

The defendant will, however, have the right to appeal against the judgment within 30 days calculated from the day following the date judgment is served on him.[6] If, however, he attended the court (even if he attended only one hearing), then the 30-day period will be calculated from the day following the date of judgment. Service of the judgment will be effected once by the court bailiff in person or at his domicile or place of work.[7]

---

[1] Article 131(1) of the Civil Procedure Law.

[2] Article 130 of the Civil Procedure Law.

[3] Supreme Court of Cassation Judgment 589 for the year 20 dated 7 February 2001.

[4] Article 53(1) of the Civil Procedure Law.

[5] Article 169 of the Civil Procedure Law.

[6] Articles 152 (1) and 159 of the Civil Procedure Law. Supreme Court of Cassation Judgment 79 for the year 19 dated 25 January 1998, Supreme Court of Cassation Judgment 74 for the year 20 dated 28 September 1999.

[7] Article 152(3) of the Civil Procedure Law.

If no appeal is filed within the 30 days, the judgment will become final and may be executed against the judgment debtor in the Execution Court under normal execution procedures. However, if the defendant is domiciled outside the jurisdiction of the court, 10 days will be added to this period and 60 days will be added if the person's domicile is outside the UAE.[1]

5.3 Judgment in the Presence of Both Parties

If the defendant or the claimant attended at least one hearing of the case but failed to attend the others, the judgment will be considered to have been delivered in the presence of both parties and will not be considered a default judgment.[2] As such, the 30-day period of appeal will start running from the day following the date the judgment was announced in court,[3] even if the full text of the judgment is not available until a few days later. No service of the judgment will be affected on the party who failed to attend the court to hear it. Either party will have the right to appeal against the judgment within the 30-day period. Failing an appeal by either party, execution proceedings will follow.

5.4 The Claimant's Failure to Attend Court

As mentioned, if the defendant failed to attend the court following a proper service of summons, the court may proceed against the defendant and deliver a default judgment. If, however, the defendant attended the court at the scheduled hearing and the claimant failed to attend, the defendant may inform the court that he would like to withdraw from the hearing. He will then be considered to be absent and the court may, if it is the first hearing, strike the case from the court records. If the request is made at a subsequent hearing the court may reserve the case for judgment or strike it from the records.[4] If the case is struck off the records no further hearing date will be scheduled for the case and the file will be taken off the court role.

The claimant does have the right to make an application to schedule another hearing for the case (upon payment of a nominal court fee) in order to restore the case onto the court role. In this instance the claimant must, within a period of three months, make an application to restore the case to

---

[1] Article 12 of the Civil Procedure Law. Supreme Court of Cassation Judgment 209 for the year 21 dated 21 February 2000, Supreme Court of Cassation Judgment 143 for the year 22 dated 31 March 2002.

[2] Supreme Court of Cassation Judgment 57 for the year 21 dated 22 November 2000.

[3] Article 152(1) of the Civil Procedure Law.

[4] Articles 51(1) and 51(2) of the Civil Procedure Law.

the court role and there will be no legal ramifications for having the case struck off other than the delay of the case.[1] A new hearing will have to be scheduled and notice must once again be served on the defendant. Again, if the defendant fails to attend after the first service, service will have to be repeated. Once the case is renewed it will be treated as if it is a new case where proper service has to be effected. A hearing date will be scheduled and the case will proceed from the point where it was terminated.

If the claimant fails to renew the case within the three-month period, it will not be possible to renew the case at a later date and the court fees will be forfeited. The claimant will have to file a new case with fresh pleadings and pay new court fees. The main action will not be considered *res judicata* by virtue of the fact that it was cancelled, but it may have consequences in regard to time bars. Once a case is filed, the time bar will be interrupted for a period of three months. If the case has not been renewed within the three-month period, the time bar will start to run again.[2]

5.5   Interim Judgments

It is possible that the Judge will make an interim judgment in certain applications on matters such as jurisdiction and the right to sue, before proceeding to the main action. However, in most cases the courts will prefer to rule on the matter as a whole. The UAE courts are reluctant to make an interim judgment on a case prior to it being reserved for judgment and a final judgment delivered. As an exception, interim judgments are only available before the final judgment under the following exceptional circumstances:

1. Appeal will not be permissible against a judgment which is delivered in the case while the case is being heard and continues to be heard by the Court of First Instance and has not yet been determined by a final judgment.
2. As an exception to the above, appeal is possible in respect of judgments delivered on a precautionary or a provisional matter such as an application for attachment[3] or judgment in an application to appoint a custodian or to liquidate a company or any other judgment in an urgent

---

[1] Article 51(3) of the Civil Procedure Law.

[2] Dubai Court of Cassation Judgment 76/95 dated 13 April 1996, Supreme Court of Cassation Judgment 85 for the year 21 dated 30 April 2000.

[3] Dubai Court of Cassation Judgment 220/95 dated 4 February 1996, Supreme Court of Cassation Judgment 611 for the year 18 dated 3 January 1999.

application filed in court.¹ Such an application if adjudicated by an interim judgment will be subject to an appeal.
3. Any judgment which suspends the hearing in the case.²
4. Any judgment which can be implemented or enforced through the execution proceedings against the defendants.
5. Any judgment delivered which determines the non-jurisdiction of the court or holds that the court has a jurisdiction to hear the matter.

Interim judgments in connection with the above matters will be delivered in a full text through the normal process signed by the court and served on the parties. However, following an interim judgment, should the court decide to proceed with the other matters of the case such as dealing with the merits of the case after determining the jurisdiction and should one of the parties fail to attend the court after the interim judgment, the party concerned must be summoned again to proceed further with the case i.e. A fresh service of summons must be effected on the party who failed to attend the court following an interim judgment, when proceeding further to deal with other issues.

5.6 Summary Judgment

The UAE legal system does not recognise a motion requesting the court to make a judgment without proceeding to trial or "summary judgment". Every action is required to proceed through the normal procedures of a main action even if there is an admission of liability prior to the action or conclusive evidence of the debt or liability. In terms of the Civil Procedure Law, however, there is one exception to this.³

A judgment can be obtained *ex parte* against a defendant for commercial debts substantiated by a commercial instrument such as a bill of exchange, promissory note or cheque, which are valid but not paid. This procedure comes under the heading "Orders for Payment" in the Civil Procedure Law in terms of which one may apply to the court for judgment against the defendant (being the drawer of the commercial instrument), *ex parte* immediately following the application, provided that the claimant provides the court with the following:⁴

---

[1] Supreme Court of Cassation Judgment 250 for the year 16 dated 10 January 1995.

[2] Dubai Court of Cassation Judgment 149/93 dated 21 November 1993.

[3] Article 143 of the Civil Procedure Law. Dubai Court of Cassation Judgment 51/95 dated 15 October 1995, Dubai Court of Cassation Judgment 183/95 dated 10 February 1996.

[4] Article 144 of the Civil Procedure Law.

1. Evidence that the claimant holds a commercial instrument in terms of which the defendant is indebted to the claimant or if the debt is a commercial debt proven by a written instrument.
2. Evidence that the claimant has served an official notice on the defendant requesting payment of the amount claimed within 5 days, and notifying him that failing which the claimant will apply for summary judgment and that the defendant has failed to pay. Such notice may be served on the defendant by registered mail or by hand in which event it is advisable to obtain an acknowledgement of receipt.
3. An application to the Judge requesting summary judgment in duplicate setting out a summary of the claim and the remedy sought from the court.

If the claimant is able to provide the abovementioned evidence, judgment will be delivered *ex parte* in his favour for the amount claimed. The defendant must be notified of the judgment within 6 months thereof, failing which the judgment will be null and void.[1] The defendant has the right to object to the judgment within 15 days.[2] If an objection is filed it will be heard by the same Judge and the action will follow the normal process before the court. If no objection is filed, the judgment will be final against the defendant.

It is at the Judge's discretion whether to grant such an order or to refer the matter to trial. If the Judge is of the opinion that the conditions for a summary judgment are not satisfied or is not inclined to give a summary judgment on the subject matter, a hearing will be scheduled for the case. The defendant will be served with a summons and the action will proceed in the normal course.

The claimant will be required to pay the court fees whether it is a summary judgment or otherwise and to file the Statement of Claim together with the documentation as with any normal action in addition to the above. The appeal procedure will apply as normal.

It should be noted that the courts rarely apply summary judgment and normally refer the case to be heard in the normal course.

---

[1] Article 146 of the Civil Procedure Law.
[2] Article 147(1) of the Civil Procedure Law.

Chapter Six

ATTACHMENTS AND URGENT APPLICATIONS

6.1 Attachments

An attachment[1] is a seizure of assets ordered by the court at the claimant's request, prior to judgment in order to preserve those assets during the trial. It is a useful tool for a creditor to ensure that the assets are not disposed of prior to judgment. Obtaining a precautionary attachment order before filing an action has always been available in the UAE. Attachment applications may also be made after an action has been filed in the same court which is hearing the main action.[2] Articles 22 and 38 of the Civil Procedure Law provide that the courts have jurisdiction to determine an urgent preliminary application for an attachment or an urgent application for a precautionary matter even if the court has no jurisdiction to hear the main action, although this is rarely applied.[3]

Normally, the defendant (judgment debtor) will not be notified of a court order for attachment unless the attachment order was made at a hearing at which he is present. Attachments are usually ordered by a Judge in an *ex parte* application.

Attachments may be filed against any assets including bank accounts, machinery, goods or other assets owned by the defendant and under his possession or owned by the defendant but in the possession of a third party.

---

[1] Article 252 of the Civil Procedure Law.
[2] Supreme Court of Cassation Judgment 50 of the year 19 dated 19 December 1997, Dubai Court of Cassation Judgment 202/99 dated 23 October 1999.
[3] Dubai Court of Cassation Judgment 194/95 dated 9 March 1996.

The claimant in the action must specify the assets, money or material to be attached before the application will be granted.[1]

The following assets cannot be attached:[2]

1. Public or private property owned by the State or the governments of any of the Emirates.
2. The house in which the judgment debtor, and his legal dependents in the case of his death, reside.
3. The debtor's necessary clothes and whatever he and his family need in their house, such as furniture, kitchen appliances, food and fuel for six months.
4. Land or agricultural equipment owned by the farmer or hunter to the extent he needs for making a living and supporting his dependents.
5. Grants or bequeathed property given so that their interest or profits may be used for temporary or life maintenance or pension, amounts adjudged by courts to be temporarily decided or judged as maintenance or to be disposed of for a certain purpose, to a quarter only in settlement of the decided maintenance.
6. Grants or bequeathed property under a pre-condition that they may not be attached if the person requiring the attachment is a creditor of the persons to whom the gift or bequest is made whose debt arose before the grant or the bequest was made, except for the debt of a decided maintenance and within the limit of a quarter.
7. Books, equipment, tools and requisites needed by the debtor for practicing his profession or craft unless the attachment was effected to collect the price or maintenance cost thereof.[3]
8. Movables considered as property by appropriation if attached in an independent manner from the property allocated to its service unless the attachment was effected to collect the price or maintenance costs thereof.
9. Wages and salaries, except to the extent of half of the basic wage or salary may be attached. Preference shall be given to maintenance debts.

The courts do not recognise the system of injunction or restraining orders and as such the attachment will only be granted against assets which can be located, identified and physically available for attachment by the court.

If the value of the assets attached exceeds the amount claimed, the Judge may, upon application by the defendant or at the court's discretion, order

---

[1] Article 254(1) of the Civil Procedure Law.

[2] Article 247 of the Civil Procedure Law.

[3] Supreme Court of Cassation Judgment 339 for the year 17 dated 25 February 1996.

the release of certain assets to the limit of the value of the amount claimed.[1] In the event of a dispute, an expert may be appointed to assess the value of the assets attached.[2]

Attachments may be granted for the full value of the claim made by the claimant and the court may assess the amount claimed by the claimant. The court may reject the application for an attachment in part and permit an attachment in part of the amount claimed. In practice, attachments are usually granted to secure a claim which is likely to be due and payable by the defendants to the claimant and are assessed qualitatively on an ad hoc basis subject to the outcome of the main action.[3]

6.1.1 Procedure

In order for the attachment to be granted, the claimant's Statement of Claim must contain the following details:

1. The facts of the case, the cause of action and the specific remedy requested. The Statement of Claim is in brief, usually no more than three to five pages;
2. The value of the claim and evidence to substantiate the value of the claim. If the debt is for an undetermined amount, the Judge may temporarily estimate the debt on the basis of the claimant's submission;[4]
3. Proof in general that there is a risk of loss of rights such as if the debtor has no stable residence in the UAE, if the creditor feels that the debtor may abscond or cancel his assets or if there is a risk of loss of collateral.[5] Basically, the claimant needs to prove that reasonable grounds exist that there is a risk that the assets may be lost;
4. Details of the defendant's assets and their location;
5. If the claim relates to the arrest of a ship, evidence must be provided to show that the debt is a marine claim and the ship is owned by the defendant or chartered to the charterer if the claim is against the charterer. If the claim relates to a trademark, evidence must be provided to show registration of the trademark locally. In any particular matter which requires special evidence, documents in support thereof must be produced before the Judge to establish the right of attachment against the defendant.

---

[1] Article 251 of the Civil Procedure Law.

[2] Supreme Court of Cassation Judgment 383 for the year 17 dated 11 February 1996.

[3] Dubai Court of Cassation Judgment 206/ 96 dated 21 December 1996.

[4] Article 254(1) of the Civil Procedure Law.

[5] Article 252(1) of the Civil Procedure Law.

All the above must be filed with the Clerk of the Court who will organise the documents in a file ready for the attachment. An attachment reference number will be provided to the claimant with a voucher for the payment of court fees. Following the payment of the court fees, the file will be registered in court and placed before a Judge to decide on the matter. Usually this process is completed on the same day in a matter of an hour or two subject to the workload of the Clerk of the Court and of the Judge. Once the attachment is registered, the specific procedure to be followed will depend on whether the attachment application is filed before or during the main action and there is a different procedure to be followed for each.

6.1.2   *Application for an Attachment Prior to the Main Action*

Once the court fees are paid and the application is registered, the file will be referred to a Judge dealing with urgent applications and attachments at the court. Normally, two or three Judges are available for urgent applications and attachments and the Clerk of the Court will allocate the file to one of these Judges on a random basis.

In Abu Dhabi and Dubai it may be possible to make an application during the morning office hours and also between 5pm to 7pm in the afternoon. The Judge will then consider the application and make a decision either to grant or reject the application. This process usually takes half an hour to an hour for the Judge to review the file and make his decision, subject to the availability of the Judge and his workload that day.

Following the order made by the Judge, the file will then be returned to the Clerk of the Court to enforce the order. In the case of an attachment of a ship and any other matter which is extremely urgent, an attachment will be enforced immediately (on the same day) even if the order was granted in the afternoon. Attachments against bank accounts, assets, warehouses or goods will be enforced on the following day and sometimes may take two to three days subject to availability of the court bailiff who will enforce the attachment order and attend to the typing process for the letters which are required to be sent to banks or other departments or courts for the enforcement of the court order.

The procedures referred to above are conducted *ex parte* and the order will be granted and enforced without the defendant being served or notified of the order delivered against him.[1] If the application is rejected, the claimant may then file an appeal or objection as the case may be.[2]

If the order is granted in favour of the claimant, the claimant ought to supervise the process of the enforcement of the attachment order with the court bailiff to ensure that the attachment is enforced immediately or as soon as possible. If, in the case of extreme urgency it becomes difficult to enforce the order immediately because of the non-availability of court bailiff or the court's workload, the matter should be brought to the attention of the Chief Justice of the court. It is advisable for the claimant to accompany the court bailiff to guide him to the whereabouts of the assets and to ensure that the attachments are enforced against the assets mentioned in the application and in the proper manner.

Once the attachment order has been granted, the claimant is required to file the main action for the substantive claim within eight days from the date upon which the attachment order is enforced and not the date upon which the order is granted.[3] If the main action is not filed within eight days of the enforcement, the attachment may be vacated and held to be null and void.[4]

The claimant may make further applications to the Judge who may grant him an attachment order to deal with the clarification of the assets or any problem that may arise compelling the claimant to request a further application for an attachment. All these applications must be made to the same Judge who granted the original order and not the court that has been hearing the main action if the main action has been filed.

The main difference between filing an attachment application before or after the filing of the main action is that such an application, objection, review or clarification to the process must be filed in the case of an application before the main action before the Judge who granted the order. The application for attachment after the main action is filed before the same court and the same panel of Judges hearing the main action.

---

[1] Article 259 of the Civil Procedure Law.

[2] Dubai Court of Cassation 209/93 dated 12 December 1993, Supreme Court of Cassation Judgment 232 of the year 19 dated 27 October 1998.

[3] Article 255(2) of the Civil Procedure Law.

[4] Dubai Court of Cassation Judgment 322/94 dated 29 January 1995, Supreme Court of Cassation Judgment 13 for the year 17 dated 3 July 1995.

6.1.3   Application for an Attachment after a Main Action is Filed

Application for an attachment after the filing of a main action can take place in various ways. Firstly, the claimant may file an application for attachment in the same application as the main action. The claimant may ask the court, as part of the remedies, to grant him an attachment as security for the main claim. After the Clerk of the Court allocates a hearing date for the main action, the same file, normally on the same day or the following day by the latest, will be placed before the court hearing the matter to decide on the urgent application for an attachment. It should be noted that this option is only available in the Federal courts and is not available in Dubai.

Secondly, the claimant may also make a separate application for an attachment after the main action has been filed and after a hearing date is scheduled, during the summons process, or after the summons has been served and the action has been progressing before the courts.

Thirdly, the claimant may make an interlocutory application to the court at the hearing of the case in the presence of the defendant, or after the case has been adjourned and at the time between the date of the adjournment and the next hearing. In such a case it will be an *ex parte* application.

In these instances, the full court fees are payable.

As mentioned, if the claim in the main action amounts to less than AED 100,000 one Judge will hear the case. If it is in excess of AED 100,000 the case will be heard by 3 Judges. The court will then make a decision either to grant or reject the attachment application and refer the matter back to the Clerk of the Court. If the attachment is granted, the Clerk of the Court will then enforce the order for attachment subject to any conditions imposed by the court. If the application is rejected, the Clerk of the Court will return the file back into the system to await the scheduling of a date of hearing for the main action.

The court may, at its discretion, decide not to deal with the application separately, but to hear the claimant's application during an adjournment of the hearing scheduled for the case in the presence of the defendants. In other words, unless there is an extreme risk that the assets may be disposed of or vacated, the courts may decide not to grant the application *ex parte* and may decide instead to afford the defendant the opportunity to respond to the application. It is advisable in such a case to make an application to the Judge explaining why the application needs to be looked into before the new hearing.

If the application is granted for an attachment order *ex parte* and the defendant learns of this either from checking his file at the court or is advised of the decision at a scheduled hearing of the main action where both parties are required to be present, the claimant is required under the law to file the main action within eight days from the date on which the order for the attachment was enforced as outlined above. However, since the claimant has already filed the main action before the court, the question arises as to whether he is required to file another action, within eight days from the date upon which the attachment was enforced. The answer to this question is rather ambiguous and the rules somewhat unclear. The rules also appear to differ between those adopted in the Federal court and those adopted in the Dubai courts and the position is, in general as follows:

1. If the action is heard before the Dubai courts and the attachment order filed before the Dubai courts, the claimant must make an application to the court within eight days or on the eighth day, after the attachment order is enforced, requesting the court to amend the Statement of Claim to include the filing of the attachment with the main action and to uphold and confirm the attachment order when the final judgment is delivered in the main action. This rule is applied even if the hearing date for the case is adjourned and falls after the 8-day period. It is likely that the court will initial the application to be heard at the hearing. At the hearing the court will acknowledge the application and will join the attachment to the court file within the main action. Accordingly, in Dubai there is no need to file another action although this procedure has however not been tested.
2. If the application is filed before the Federal courts, a new action must be filed within eight days of the enforcement of the attachment order <u>in addition</u> to the main action. Court fees will have to be paid and the Statement of Claim and supporting documents must be filed according to the standard procedure.[1] This new action is intended only to secure the attachment order and in the new action, in addition to the remedies requested in the main action, the following remedies will be requested:
    a) To uphold and confirm the attachment order delivered in favour of the claimant;
    b) To join the attachment with the main action for judgment simultaneously;

---

[1] Supreme Court of Cassation Judgment 86 for the year 17 dated 3 July 1995, Supreme Court of Cassation Judgment 50 for the year 19 dated 9 December 1997, Supreme Court of Cassation Judgment 436 for the year 19 dated 15 June 1999.

c) That the attachment in the main action be upheld, a favourable judgment delivered in favour of the claimant and an order for the payment of the court fees and costs of such an action, (unless the judgment is proportionate and therefore proportionate court fees should be awarded).

At the first hearing following the enforcement of the attachment order (or the filing of the main action in the case of an attachment granted before the Federal court), the court will join the attachment with the main action. If the claimant objects or the defendant challenges the court's order, the court will usually deal with the objection independently of the main action. Thus, the courts may deal with the objection at the same hearing as the main action and within the same process as the main action, however this is not common. Because of the urgent nature of attachments, the courts may (and often do) deal with an application for objection against the attachment separately from the main action. Therefore a party may file two parallel hearings, one for the main action and one for the attachment, though the main action is unlikely to be determined and reserved for judgment before the objection against the attachment is decided upon. Also, relatively speaking, the process of the attachment is usually speedier than that of the main action.

Other than the above, all the procedures relating to attachment orders including objection, enforcement, dealing with clarifications, applications, or further attachment applications made by the claimant, will follow the same procedure as an application filed before the main action, with the exception that such an application and process will be dealt with by the court hearing the main action rather than the Judge in charge of attachments and urgent applications at the courts. This is only at the level of the Court of First Instance.

6.2 Objection to an Attachment Order

Both the claimant and the defendant have the right to object. In the case of the claimant, he may object against the quantum of the attachments or against the fact that the Judge may have granted the remedy in part but not all, or not to the extent requested. The claimant may therefore request further attachments provided that what he is asking for was contained in his original application. The defendant may object to the actual attachment that was ordered, or he may request the court to vacate, vary or ease the attachments upon the grounds which he will put to the court.[1]

---

[1] Supreme Court of Cassation Judgment 246 for the year 19 dated 31 March 1998.

6.2.1 Objection by the Claimant

The claimant can file an objection against any process relating to the order granted with regard to an attachment, any conditions set out therein, or any process relating to the order, to which the claimant has a grievance. The claimant shall object to the same Judge or court who rejected his application either in full or in part or if a specific condition was imposed for the enforcement of the attachment order granted in favour of the claimant,[1] such as to lodge a bank guarantee or other security which the claimant believes is unreasonable. An objection against an order can be filed directly with the Clerk of the Court by a simple application and detailed memorandum together with supporting documents.[2]

A hearing date will be scheduled to hear the claimant's objection to the attachment. Both parties will be informed of the hearing and service will take place once and not twice as in the case of a normal action. Objection to an attachment will take place separately before the Judge who is giving the order or before the court involved in the main action if the main action has been filed and the order was rejected by the court in the first place. The defendant will be afforded the opportunity to respond and may file a memorandum together with supporting documents in connection with the objection. Objections will not be heard *ex parte*.

The objection process may go through a number of hearings before being reserved for judgment. As such, there will be no element of surprise involved in attaching the defendant's assets even if the objection filed by the claimant was accepted and an order for an attachment is granted in favour of the claimant. If the court grants the claimant's application for an objection and revises its original order and grants a full attachment as originally requested in the main application, it will then be enforced immediately through the normal procedure for attachment orders. It will not be possible for the defendant to halt the process of the enforcement of the order which was granted in the objection process even if he filed an objection or an appeal and in principle, the order is good for immediate enforcement, irrespective of any objection or appeal.

The claimant, however, cannot request a remedy that is different or more than what he originally requested in the main application. Such a request will be considered to be a new application and should not be applied for

---

[1] Dubai Court of Cassation Judgment 71/93 dated 10 July 1993.

[2] Dubai Court of Cassation Judgment 98/92 dated 23 May 1992, Dubai Court of Cassation Judgment 126/94 dated 15 May 1994, Dubai Court of Cassation Judgment 135/94 dated 12 November 1994, Dubai Court of Cassation Judgment 302/95 dated 7 April 1995.

through the objection process. He also cannot rely on new grounds which were not the subject of his original application although he can file new evidence relevant to the matter. The Dubai Court of Cassation has also held that the claimant in his objection may not file further documents which were not filed in his main application.[1]

6.2.2 The Defendant's Objection

If the Court of the First Instance awards an order to the claimant in full or in part, and the defendant finds out about the attachment at the first hearing of the case, he may file an objection to the attachment at any time, without limitation or time bar. The defendant may object to the nature of the attachment on legal grounds or on the merits of the attachment or the quantum attached, the defendant may also apply to the court to substitute another asset for the assets attached.

The defendant's objection will be filed in the same manner as that in which the claimant filed his objection against the attachment order. An application must be made to the Clerk of the Court in a simple application with a detailed memorandum together with the supporting documents. A standard fee will be charged for the objection and a hearing date will be scheduled to which the claimant will be summoned once to attend the court to respond to the defendant's objection to the attachment order.

Following an exchange of memoranda and documents, the court will deliver an order in relation to the objection filed by the defendant. The court may make one of the following orders:

1. To lift the attachments ordered originally by the court and cancel all the letters sent to the other courts or the banks to inform them of the lifting of the attachments and vacate its effect in totality.
2. To amend the attachment order by transferring the attachment to other assets or to limit it to a particular asset such as to the nature of the attachment or the value of the assets.
3. To reject the defendant's objection in whole or in part and uphold the court's attachment order.
4. To reject the claimant's objection and uphold the order rejecting the attachment.

While the case is being heard, the attachment will be enforced and any order granted in terms of 1, 2 or 3 above shall be enforced immediately irrespective of any appeal filed by either party.

---

[1] Dubai Court of Cassation Judgment 224/2000 dated 24 September 2000.

6.3 Appeal

If either the claimant or the defendant has any objection to the attachment, in full or in part, they have the right to appeal against the court's decision. On appeal however, the court will not only consider and review the objection process but also the attachment order or the main order granting or rejecting the attachment application as the case may be. The Court of Appeal will review the attachment order in its totality from both the factual and the legal perspective.

An appeal by either party may be made by an application to the Court of Appeal. The appeal consists of a memorandum of appeal in detail with supporting documentation or in a brief filed in court, setting out the grounds of the appeal and the remedy required. A further detailed memorandum of appeal may be filed by the appellants at the first hearing of the appeal or later, along with supporting documentation. Respondents to the appeal may also file a memorandum together with supporting documentation.

No witnesses are permitted in the case of an objection to an attachment or an appeal against an attachment as this is an urgent application.

Irrespective of the appeal, the court order for an attachment or vacation of the attachment will be enforced and an appeal against the court's decision in the objection process will not suspend the courts' order in the objection process while the appeal is being heard. If, for example, the attachment is lifted, the court will proceed with the lifting of the attachment in vacating the attachments in totality as ordered by the court in connection with the objection process whether an appeal was filed or not. Similarly, if an attachment was granted the judgment will be enforced whether an appeal was filed or not. The Appeal Court has the power to suspend the decisions of the Court of First Instance, at either party's request, however, the court rarely exercises such power.

Naturally, if the Court of Appeal cancels the judgment delivered by the Court of First Instance in connection with the attachment, the attachments will be vacated or changed in accordance with the Court of Appeal's decision and such an order will be enforced immediately.

The parties may appeal against the Court of Appeal's decision to the Court of Cassation in Dubai and, if the matter is a Federal matter to the Supreme Court of Cassation of the Federal court. Again, appealing to the court of Cassation will not suspend the enforcement of the Court of Appeal's decision. However, an appeal to the Court of Cassation will be on a point of law only and no arguments, facts or documents may be put before the Court of Cassation.

The Court of Cassation's judgment will be final and will be enforced immediately by the lower courts. If the Court of Cassation has cancelled the attachment order that was upheld throughout, the attachment will be lifted immediately. If the Court of Cassation, on the other hand, has confirmed an attachment order which was rejected by the Court of First Instance and Appeal, the courts will enforce the attachment immediately and no further objection or appeal is possible.

All attachments are enforced by the execution department of the Court of First Instance and not at the Appeal or the Cassation Courts, even if the order was delivered by the Court of Appeal or Cassation, since the Court of First Instance supervises the execution process.

In Dubai, it is possible to appeal against the court's attachment order directly to the Court of Appeal without having to file an objection first.[1] In other words, if the attachment application was rejected or an attachment has been granted and enforced, either the claimant or the defendant in Dubai has a choice either:

1. To file an objection, first before the same Judge who ordered the first decision at the Court of First Instance and then file an appeal against the decision made in the objection, or
2. To appeal directly to the Court of Appeal, appealing against the Judge's first decision without having to file an objection in the first place.

However, in Abu Dhabi, the appeal in such circumstances will be dismissed in its form as the court requires that the party must first file an objection and after the decision is made regarding the objection, only then can an appeal be filed against the objection decision and not the first decision made by the court.[2]

A party may file further attachment applications as circumstances may change from time to time. There is no limitation to this right even if a decision has been made on appeal.

---

[1] Dubai Court of Cassation Judgment 209/93 dated 12 December 1993

[2] Supreme Court of Cassation Judgment 315 for the year 15 dated 30 April 1995..

6.4   Enforcement of Attachment Orders

Once the attachment order is granted by the Court of the First Instance or granted at the hearing of the objection or upheld by the Court of Appeal or Cassation, enforcement of the attachment must be executed by order of the Clerk of the Court through a bailiff, and the Execution Department of the Court of First Instance.

The Judge may prescribe conditions for the enforcement such as some form of proof of ownership of certain assets which are the subject of the attachment or a copy of a licence to prove that the business to be attached is owned by the defendant or a guarantee which the Judge has ordered the claimant to put up as a security for an attachment.

In normal circumstances and in most applications for attachment, a bank guarantee or security from the claimant is not required. The court usually grants an attachment against the defendant's assets whether a vessel, bank accounts, or other goods, without the need of having security for damages. It is however at the discretion of the Judge to order the claimant to lodge a bank guarantee for an amount assessed by the court or to require an undertaking by a third party to cover any damages that may be suffered by the defendant should the action prove to be unjustified. Under the UAE trademark law, however, attachment against counterfeit goods or look alike goods can only be granted upon deposit of security to the court or a bank guarantee[1]. In an application to impound a passport or to prevent someone from leaving the country, security in the form of a bank guarantee will be required.[2] The amount of security that will be required will be assessed by the court and will differ from case to case. In Dubai, the court may require, in rare circumstances, security for the arrest of a ship to cover port or other incidental charges while the ship is under arrest.

In other instances where there are attachments against particular assets which require certain clarification such as a business which requires to show the owner of the business, or motor vehicles which require evidence that the vehicle is owned by defendant, the court may order the claimant to show evidence that the assets which he seeks to attach are actually registered and owned by the defendant. In these circumstances the court may, on application by the claimant, assist the claimant if he has no access to such information, by writing to certain government departments such as

---

[1] Article 41(2) of the Trademark Law, Federal Law no 37 of 1992.

[2] Supreme Court of Cassation Judgment 15 for the year 15 dated 30 January 1994, Dubai Court of Cassation Judgment 345/1994 dated 25 March 1995, Dubai Court of Cassation Judgment 303/96 dated 11 May 1997, Dubai Court of Cassation Judgment 350/98 dated 21 November 1998.

the traffic police or to the Company Registrar to obtain relevant information as such information is not usually open to the public. In general, however, it is not easy to obtain information about the financial status and assets of companies and individuals in the UAE.

Once the Clerk of the Court is satisfied that the conditions (if any) have been met, he will then forward the file to the execution court to enforce the attachment.

Once the file reaches the execution department the Clerk of the Execution Court will:

1. Write letters to relevant government departments or private entities where an attachment can be imposed by correspondence.[1] If the attachment involves bank accounts or the money is held by a third party, a letter will be forwarded to the banks or such party advising them of the attachment, requesting them to attach the money or the assets and to confirm to the court by return. In this instance, the party holding the assets will be considered to be the custodian of the assets or money by order of the court and is answerable to the court for those assets or money.
2. If the assets are tangible and are physically located in a warehouse, office, or in the hands of a third party and require the appointment of a custodian, the Clerk of the Court will schedule a time to enforce the attachments. He would normally be available from 7.00 am to 6.00 pm to enforce the attachments and usually effects the attachment one or two days after the receipt of the file. In case of immediate urgency where there is a risk of the assets being disposed of or moved, the matter may be put to the Judge or the Chief Justice of the court for immediate action.
3. If the Clerk of the Court anticipates any difficulties in enforcing the attachment (i.e. the declaration is ambiguous or the location is not clear), he will seek clarification of such information from the claimant or the Judge before proceeding with the attachment against the assets.

6.4.1   Attachment Minutes

A copy of all the correspondence with regard to the attachment will be retained in the attachment file.[2] During the enforcement of the order the court bailiff will note down all the process, details of the goods attached, the location and the address. The court bailiff and the parties present at the

---

[1] Article 263(2) of the Civil Procedure Law.

[2] Article 271(1) of the Civil Procedure Law.

attachment will sign the "attachment minutes." If the attachment involves trinkets, gold bars, or any other precious metal, jewellery or precious stones, artwork or valuable items, an expert will be appointed by the execution Judge at the request of the claimant or debtor, to weigh and describe the assets for insertion in the attachment minutes.[1]

6.4.2 The Custodian

If the goods are secured, the court bailiff will retain the key. However, if the goods cannot be secured, or they are located in an area where they are mixed with other assets and goods, a custodian must be appointed to guard the goods on behalf of the court.[2] The custodian must sign a declaration confirming his appointment as custodian for the goods attached and give an undertaking that he will not dispose or remove the goods without an order from the court. Normally, the custodian appointed is a representative of the defendant, at the defendant's premises and his identity card or passport may be held by the court unless a Judge decides otherwise. The custodian will be personally responsible to the court for those goods. The claimant may object to the court regarding the identity of the custodian or the manner in which the goods are stored or used and he may also ask the court to secure the assets in another fashion at his cost.

The party who is ordered to attach assets or money he holds for the defendant, must confirm to the court the status of the money and the availability of the money and the quantum within 7 days, failing which such party may be held personally liable and he may be joined in the main action for failing to respond.[3]

It is possible, at the Judge's discretion, to change the custodian from time to time by nominating another person. It is also possible but only at the Judge's discretion, for a custodian to resign.[4] If a custodian resigns, the defendant will be asked to appoint another custodian as a replacement failing which, the claimant will be appointed as custodian for the goods. The goods may be moved by order of the Judge and stored in a warehouse and either the claimant or the defendant will be ordered to bear the costs. If no custodian is available, the court may close down the premises and retain the keys pending the outcome of the case.[5]

---

[1] Articles 272(1) and 272(2) of the Civil Procedure Law.

[2] Articles 273 and 274 of the Civil Procedure law.

[3] Article 263(1) of the Civil Procedure Law.

[4] Article 277(1) of the Civil Procedure Law.

[5] Dubai Court of Cassation Judgment 313/2001 dated 10 November 2001.

Any application relating to the appointment of the custodian, the removal of the custodian, the fact that the custodian is not fit to act as custodian, or if he has disposed of the goods or where there is a risk that he may do so, must be put in writing to the Judge. If the custodian breaches his duty, he could be subject to both civil and criminal sanction.

6.4.3 Problems in Attachment

If, during the enforcement of the attachment, the court bailiff suspects that the goods about to be attached are not the same as those described in the application, or that the goods are located in a warehouse or yard which does not bear the name of the defendant and therefore there is a risk that the goods may not be owned by the defendant, or should a third party claim that the goods are owned by him and not by the defendant, then the court bailiff must immediately put this matter in writing to the Judge to ask his permission for the appropriate action that the Judge believes the court bailiff should take to secure the attachment of the goods. In addition, if the court bailiff has difficulty in accessing the premises or the premises are locked and requires the lock to be broken, he must immediately advise the Judge in writing for his immediate decision.

The Judge will review the report made by the court bailiff and any comments that the claimant may make to clarify the situation, and will then make one of the following orders:

1. To order the claimant to clarify the situation and provide evidence of the ownership of the warehouse or the premises and any matter that the Judge believes that the claimant needs to address before enforcing the attachment further.
2. To order the bailiff to suspend the attachment and not to take any further action as it may become evident to the Judge that the goods that were about to be attached do not belong to the defendant and it is difficult to ascertain who is actually the owner.
3. To order the court bailiff to proceed with the attachment according to the guidelines and the decision made by the court, including breaking into the premises or changing the lock or by use of the police force to enter the premises or to move the goods to another warehouse depending upon the circumstances.

The correspondence between the court bailiff and the Judge with regard to the enforcement process of the attachment may take one to two days before a final decision is made and the proper action taken. All the above processes will take place in the absence of the defendant unless of course, the defendant interferes in the process and approaches the Judge and the court bailiff with an objection or an application to clarify his own position with regard to the enforcement process.

6.4.4 Third Party Challenge

In terms of the Civil Procedure Law, any party who has a grievance in respect of the attachment process may file an application to the court challenging the process or part of it, on the grounds that the goods attached are owned by another party, or the attachment is not properly conducted, or any other matter relating to the process or the enforcement of the attachment.

A recent decision indicated that if a person who is not a party to the proceedings has an interest or an objection he must file a new action in order to suspend the sale of the assets.[1]

A challenging application is different from the objection since it does not deal with the merits or the substance of the attachment but with the enforcement of the attachment process itself through to the execution process.

Challenging the process can be filed at any time during the attachment or thereafter verbally to the court bailiff noted down on the minutes of the attachment records, or by separate application to the court upon payment of a nominal court fee. The challenging application may be filed either by the claimant or the defendant and will be heard immediately by the Judge or through a hearing process. If the Judge decides to hear the application (which is often the case) a hearing date will be scheduled and both parties will be invited to attend the court to deal with the challenging application. This may take a few hearings during which the parties can exchange documents and memoranda and thereafter, the Judge will reserve the case for judgment. The decision of the court may be challenged by an application to the Court of Appeal by either party but is not subject to any further appeal to the Court of Cassation.[2]

---

[1] Supreme Court of Cassation Judgment 246 for the year 19 dated 31 March 1998, Dubai Court of Cassation Judgment 306/2001 dated 18 November 2001.

[2] Article 161 of the Civil Procedure Law.

In either case, the challenging application will not suspend the enforcement of the attachment order although it is unlikely that any further attachment order may be granted by the Judge while the challenging the application is being heard. In other words the court bailiff will proceed with the enforcement of the attachment, as originally ordered by the court, but it is unlikely that the court will grant the claimant any further remedy for attachment of any other assets or a request to obey the orders until the challenging application is fully determined by the courts.

6.5 Sale of Attached Assets

In principle, there is no law or condition prohibiting a Judge from ordering the sale of goods under attachment before judgment on the merits of the case. However, in practice, goods under attachment are not sold until final judgment if the defendant has failed to pay the amount awarded by the court after being given proper notice to do so.[1] In these circumstances, the goods will be sold by public auction through the process set out in the Civil Procedure Law.[2]

It is not possible to apply to court to sell the goods before the judgment is delivered in favour of the claimant. If the goods are kept as a security for the amount claimed, the court is in no position to sell the goods before the judgment is delivered in favour of the claimant. However, if the goods are perishable and the date of expiry is approaching, it may be possible to apply to a Judge to order the defendants either to replace the goods or the material or the court may do so, before the judgment in the matter. While this is possible in principle, in practice it is rather difficult due to the technical procedures involved. Furthermore, the defendant could instigate an appeal process which would make the application ineffective. The sale of assets before judgment will not be an option in the case of real estate property.

6.6 Attachment of Land[3]

An attachment order for real estate property before the judgment is delivered is not possible under the UAE law. Therefore, attachment and the sale of land is only possible if the claimant holds a final judgment to secure

---

[1] However, the Court may order the sale of goods or assets before judgment especially if it was mortgaged according to Article 453 of the Commercial Code.

[2] Articles 282 and 295 of the Civil Procedure Law.

[3] Article 292 of the Civil Procedure Law. Dubai Court of Cassation Judgment 92/93 dated 23 May 1993, Dubai Court of Cassation Judgment 377/94 dated 16 March 1996.

recovery of a judgment already delivered in his favour. A precautionary attachment against real estate property is not possible though it may be possible (although rarely offered by the court) to apply to the court to attach the income generated out of the property or a building, in other words rent and income generated out of the real estate property but not the actual property itself.[1]

6.7 Disposing of the Assets Before the Order is Enforced

The UAE law provides for the attachment of assets provided that the claimant locates those assets and specifies them in the application of the attachment order, by order delivered *ex parte* in the absence of the defendants. However, if the defendant disposes of the assets, relocates them or moves them before the orders are enforced, there is no legal recourse against the defendant whether civil or criminal. In other words, if the defendant came to know of the order delivered by the courts and before such an order was served on him officially or before the goods were attached by the court, he disposes of the goods or transfers them elsewhere, there will be no recourse available to the claimant. The defendant will only be responsible or liable after the order of the attachment process is officially served on him or the goods actually attached and official records noted by the court bailiff. There is also no particular duty on the defendant to co-operate with the court for the enforcement of the court order other than giving access to the court bailiff to enter the premises and to provide the court bailiff with the information or details requested. Therefore, defendants often sit back and do very little to assist in the enforcement of the court order unless officially requested to do so.

The only exception to this approach is if the assets were disposed of while the defendant is insolvent and done for the purpose of denying creditors the right to recover their debts. While one cannot attach these assets one may file a case through the normal process to rescind such a transaction on the grounds of bad faith. Another exception is if the disposal takes place while the matter has been challenged in the Appeal Courts.

---

[1] Private property is considered to be important in the UAE. See Article 21 of the Constitution "Private property shall be protected, conditions relating hereto shall be laid down by law. No one shall be deprived of his private property except in circumstances dictated by the public benefit in accordance with the provisions of the law and of payment of just compensation."

6.8   Urgent Applications

There are other urgent applications that a party may apply to the court for other than the attachment order. The law provides for an urgent court action where a party requests the court to give judgment in an urgent matter which requires urgent proceedings. Such proceedings are appropriate in cases where the claimant is requesting the court to appoint a liquidator, custodian or to call witnesses. Such cases are filed in the normal manner although a hearing will be scheduled within days. In some instances, these are dealt with *ex parte* and on other occasions the defendant is asked to respond. Normally such applications are dealt with on an urgent basis by the same Judge who is dealing with the attachment order and judgment is usually delivered in a speedy manner. The following urgent applications are available to the parties:

6.8.1   Application to Survey or Document Status[1]

Under the UAE Law, it is possible to file an urgent application to the court (in the same way as filing an action as indicated above) asking the court urgently to appoint a surveyor or an expert or an independent party to survey and look into urgent matters which need to be documented and surveyed before circumstances change. For example, if a ship is leaving port and the damage must be surveyed before the ship departs or if there is a danger that the goods may perish or circumstances may change because of time or condition, or for the resolution of an urgent matter in the construction industry.[2]

Under normal circumstances the courts will serve notice on the other party involved in the matter to hear the parties arguments on an urgent basis. The case may be adjourned on a day-to-day or weekly basis before the court decides on appointing an expert as the party requested or to reject the application according to the case's requirements, evidence or the facts of the case. The speed with which the matter is dealt with depends on the nature of the matter and the circumstances.

No remedies will be granted in this case other than documenting the facts or the status of the matter through the court or independent expert. The case will end with the evidence documented in court. Essentially, the court will direct the expert, arrange for the parties to meet and hear the arguments of

---

[1] Article 68(1) of the Law of Evidence

[2] Dubai Court of Cassation Judgment 410/2000 dated 28 January 2001.

both parties or any comments they may have or to reject or give an order to register the report as part of the court documents.

The evidence documented in accordance with this procedure may be used in another action where the claimant or the defendant may claim a remedy based on the facts and evidence gathered in the urgent application.

This action is normally heard on an urgent basis and a nominal court fee is charged. The Judge in charge of urgent cases will hear the case even if the amount involved is more than AED 100,000.

Judgment in this case may be appealed to the Court of Appeal although the appeal will be based on a technical matter (limited to the findings of the expert) since the Court of First Instance is merely granting a remedy to document the facts of the case.

6.8.2 Application for a Witness to be heard Prior to the Main Action[1]

Either party may make an application for a witness to be heard prior to the filing of the main action if such party believes that the witness needs to be brought before the court either because the circumstances may change or because the witness will not be available at the time when the action is filed.

There will be no claim for a remedy in such an application, which is filed in the normal course, the only claim will be to ask the court to hear the statement of the witness. The matter will be put before the Judge who is in charge of hearing urgent applications, notice of the application will be served on the other party and the witness may be called and heard before the court.

It is at the discretion of the Judge whether to hear the witness or not, and if the Judge decides to hear the witness following the submission of both parties, it will be considered on an urgent basis and a hearing will be scheduled to hear the witness in the presence of both parties. The court will document the statement of the witness and the action will end at this stage. There will be no further proceedings or events that may take place in this action other than of course hearing the statement of the witness by the court. The statement may then be used as evidence in the future action although the statement will be assessed by the courts that hear the merits of the case in due course. This kind of action will only be entertained in very

---

[1] Article 47 of the Law of Evidence.

exceptional circumstances. Nominal court fees will be charged for such an application which will be assessed by the Judge.

6.8.3 Deputation from Another Court to hear a Witness or to order a Party to Produce Documents[1]

There is a procedure available under UAE Law for the courts in the UAE to be deputed by a foreign court either to hear a statement of a witness or to order a party to produce documents. Such an application is considered and assessed by the Chief Justice of the Court. For the application to proceed, which is only in very exceptional circumstances, the court may decide to schedule a hearing, hear the statement of the witness or order the party, if appropriate under the UAE law, to exhibit certain documents as required by the petitioner. The court will then forward the statement and documents as exhibited to the court requesting the petition.

This application is however only granted in limited circumstances and is at the discretion of the Chief Justice and as such the procedure may vary from one Emirate to another. The procedure will only be entertained with a country that has a reciprocal agreement with the UAE.

6.8.4 Application to Appoint a Custodian[2]

In certain circumstances, such as:

1. assets which require special care;
2. assets which may perish if not taken care of;
3. there is a dispute over the assets pending the outcome of the civil proceedings;
4. there is a dispute between the partners of a company and the dispute has a written extent where they cannot agree on the management of the company;
5. in the case of assets which require special care and the parties involved cannot agree as to who should take of the assets or if neither of them is willing to take custody of the assets;

---

[1] In terms of reciprocal agreements with other countries.
[2] Article 29 of the Civil Procedure Law.

then either party who has an interest in preserving the assets may apply to the court for the appointment of a custodian.[1]

An application to appoint a custodian may be made to court by a simple application accompanied by the relevant documents setting out the grounds why custodian should be appointed for the assets or the company as the case may be. A court will ask the other party to the proceedings to attend court and will hear both parties' arguments and submissions on an urgent basis. The case is usually heard on a weekly basis until the case is reserved for judgment. It is up to the court to assess the extent of the urgency and grant such an application only in extreme cases where there are assets or the company is in extreme risk.

The court will either appoint a custodian who may be one of the experts listed at the court, or an independent party, an auditor or even the claimant if the court thinks the claimant is the most appropriate person to be appointed as the custodian.

Once appointed by the court, the custodian will have the full management of the assets or of the company and will be the only authorised custodian of the assets or of the company answerable only to the court. He will have the power to manage the assets, manage the company and to spend or safeguard the company's money.

The custodian will be appointed by the courts for an unlimited period and will be required by the court to file a report on a monthly basis. He may be removed from his custodianship if both parties agree or by order of the court if the circumstances which led to his appointment change. The custodian will be paid a fee to be assessed by the court and paid to him on a monthly basis by either the party to the action or from the income of the company if it is the company who has appointed him. The custodian has no power to sell or dispose of the assets unless the courts agree, he only has the right to manage and safeguard the property for the court and in the interest of both parties.

The custodian will take no instructions from either party to the action and he will only be answerable to the court. He will also be liable for gross negligence and misconduct as he may be sued by either party for such default.

---

[1] Dubai Court of Cassation Judgment 227/99 dated 14 November 1999, Dubai Court of Cassation Judgment 506/99 dated 2 April 2000, Dubai Court of Cassation Judgment 407/2000 dated 28 January 2001, Dubai Court of Cassation Judgment 351/2001 dated 30 December 2001.

The application for the appointment of a custodian will be heard by the Judge in charge of urgent applications and not by a panel of Judges even if the amount exceeds AED 100,000. There will be no remedy granted in this action other than the appointment of the custodian. If either party to the action has a claim for other remedies such as the liquidation of the company or a claim for damages, a separate action must be filed on the merits. Any claim that the custodian may have against either party such as the clarification of the situation or any additional fee that he may wish to claim must be put to the court and not to a party in the action.

The applicant bears the cost of the custodian unless the court orders otherwise. The appointment will end once the court decides and makes an order concerning the future of the assets. For the court to grant this application there must be urgency and some risk in leaving the assets under the control of either party.

Chapter Seven

EXECUTION PROCEEDINGS

7.1 Execution[1]

A judgment cannot be executed unless it has become final and is certified by the Execution Court as being good for execution. The execution procedure takes place in a separate department of the court, separate from the day-to-day dealings of the Clerks of the Court. There are Judges specifically assigned to the Execution Court[2] assisted by an execution bailiff and administrative staff at the Execution Department to administer the execution and enforcement of judgments and orders. The Executive Judge is in charge of all execution matters as well as any objections thereto.[3]

A matter will be put before an Executive Court Judge for an order to proceed with the execution of a judgment. If the judgment relates to an urgent application or an application for a precautionary attachment, the Execution Court will enforce the judgment immediately, without reference to the judgment debtor.[4]

The Execution Courts are in charge of the following:

1. Implementing and enforcing a final judgment delivered on the merits of the case to assist the claimant in enforcing the remedy that he has been awarded against the defendants.
2. The Executive Judge may look into any difficult objections or procedural issues that may arise when enforcing a final judgment delivered in favour of either party.

---

[1] Article 219ff of the Civil Procedure Law.

[2] Article 220 of the Civil Procedure Law.

[3] Dubai Court of Cassation Judgment 435/97 dated 26 April 1998.

[4] Supreme Court of Cassation Judgment 161 for the year 15 dated 12 June 1994.

3. To attach property, land or any other assets that can be located, against the judgment debtors to satisfy the judgment obtained in favour of the claimant and to assist in selling those assets by auction and to pay the proceeds of the sale to the claimant.[1]
4. To assist the claimant who has obtained a favourable judgment in repossession of assets, for delivery of an item or specific performance and supervise such a process to ensure that such delivery or possession are carried out smoothly and in an effective manner.
5. Implementing and enforcing any attachment order delivered by the courts to ensure that the attachment is enforced immediately following the order and to look into any difficulties or issues that may arise in enforcing such an attachment order delivered by the courts.[2]
6. To assist and supervise from time to time the enforcement of any order delivered on an urgent basis whether for the appointment of an expert or custodian or any matter which needs to be implemented through courts or supervised by the courts.
7. Receive payments from the judgment debtor and to release payments received to the judgment creditor.
8. Attach any assets which can be located to satisfy the judgment obtained in favour of the claimant who wishes to enforce the judgment through execution.
9. Look into any objection filed against execution proceedings or any action taken by the parties or the Court of the Execution Department and to review the execution process and to make the appropriate decision. Such an objection may be raised by the judgment debtor or any other third party that may have been affected by the execution proceedings.[3]

7.2 Procedure

Once a judgment becomes final and the judgment debtor fails to pay the amounts claimed or fails to take the appropriate action to satisfy the judgment delivered against him, the judgment creditor may apply to the Execution Court through the Execution Department to enforce the judgment against the defendant. This is regardless of whether the judgment provides for a monetary remedy or specific performance.

The application must be made to the Execution Department setting out a summary of the judgment delivered, the remedy which was granted by the

---

[1] Supreme Court of Cassation Judgment 52 for the year 18 dated 28 May 1996.

[2] Article 220 of the Civil Procedure Law.

[3] Dubai Court of Cassation Judgment 365/98 dated 2 May 1999, Dubai Court of Cassation Judgment 541/99 dated 16 April 2000.

court and the judgment creditor's request to the court to enforce the judgment in their favour. The application is usually in brief and does not extend beyond two pages unless it is accompanied by a copy of the judgment certified as final and good for execution.

The clerk at the Execution Court will thereupon open an execution file and allocate an execution number to the matter. The execution fees payable vary between the different Emirates.[1]

Once the execution file has been opened and a file number allocated, the court bailiff will serve a notice on the judgment debtor requesting him to pay the amount adjudged or to carry out the order granted by the courts within 15 days, failing which action will be taken against him by the Execution Court without further notice.[2] No execution action will be enforced by the court without this notice.

7.2.1 Notice

Notice of the execution proceedings follows the same procedures as those for service of summons as outlined above, however notice is only required to be given once to the judgment debtor and there will be no hearing date scheduled.

7.2.2 Application

The judgment debtor is merely requested to comply with the judgment failing which he will face sanction from the court. If no payment is received from the judgment debtor or should he fail to comply with the judgment in the absence of any challenging proceedings filed, the judgment creditor may after 15 days,[3] make an application to the Execution Court requesting the court to do one or all of the following:[4]

1. To sell the assets that have been attached by the court before the action, in order to satisfy the judgment delivered in favour of the claimant.
2. To attach the defendants' assets and bank accounts or any other property including real estate property which may be attached by the court at this stage.

---

[1] See Appendix 1.
[2] Article 239 of the Civil Procedure Law.
[3] Article 239(2) of the Civil Procedure Law.
[4] Supreme Court of Cassation Judgment 32 for the year 18 dated 12 November 1996.

3. To cash any amount deposited with the court as security against the claim or to serve notice on the guarantor who has guaranteed the debt on behalf of the defendants in the proceedings, if any.
4. To write letters to certain banks, departments such as the Lands Department or any other institution whether in the private sector or government sector inquiring about any assets, money or real estate property that is owned or registered in the name of the defendant and which may be free for attachment in the UAE or in a particular Emirate.

The court may grant all or some of the above applications made by the claimant in order to satisfy the judgment delivered in his favour and to assist him in recovering the amount claimed or to reach a remedy which he has been awarded. Furthermore, the court will usually grant the claimant any reasonable request including an order to search the defendant's assets provided the request and the application is specific and founded upon reasonable grounds.

For instance, the court may grant the claimant leave to investigate whether a motor vehicle is registered in the name of the defendant at the traffic police and property registered in the name of the defendant at the Lands Department, or to investigate any accounts that the defendant may hold. If certain assets are located, the court will attach the assets before auctioning them. The auction will not be granted unless the assets are first located, attached and put in the hands of a custodian. There is however no limit as to the number of applications the claimant (judgment creditor) may file until he recovers the judgment debt in full.

7.3　Challenging the Execution Proceedings

While the execution procedure may appear straightforward, in practice it is time consuming and complicated because of the rights of the judgment debtor to challenge the proceedings.

It may be possible for the judgment debtor to challenge the execution proceedings immediately following the receipt of the notice or at any time after the proceedings are initiated against him following an attachment order or otherwise.[1] Challenging the execution proceedings will follow the same procedures as challenging an attachment order set out above.[2]

---

[1] Dubai Court of Cassation Judgment 158/95 dated 28 January 1996.

[2] Articles 244 and 246 of the Civil Procedure Law.

The judgment debtor at the time of the execution may challenge the procedure by submitting an application to the court bailiff followed up by an application to court, challenging the execution proceedings on whatever grounds he feels the execution proceedings are not appropriate or alleging that they are being executed against the wrong party. Following the payment of the court fees the court will serve notice upon the judgment creditor to attend the court to respond to the challenge proceedings.

It is likely that the challenging proceedings will involve several hearings before the case is reserved for judgment. Any judgment delivered may be appealed to the Court of Appeal but not to the Court of Cassation. The appeal will be limited to the execution procedure and the judgment and not to the merits of the case. This procedure is very often used simply to delay the execution process and to prevent the judgment creditor from receiving payment of the judgment debt.[1]

Any issue relating to the execution of the judgment (not the merits as these have already been adjudicated), may be challenged through this proceedings. Thus execution against the wrong party, the wrong assets or through the wrong process may be challenged in the courts. The matter will be heard by the Executive Judge who will decide whether to proceed with the execution, leave the attachments if an attachment has already been ordered, suspend the execution, declare that the execution is null and void because it has been executed against wrong party or proceed with the execution as normal and reject the challenge filed by the judgment debtor or any other party.[2]

The proceedings do not necessarily need to be filed by the judgment debtor, it may be filed by any party against whom the execution is directed. In certain circumstances, an interested party may not challenge the procedure by objection. A separate action must be brought to prove one's title to the goods and to nullify the attachment.

The proceedings to challenge the application for execution will suspend the execution proceedings and no further action can be taken in the execution proceedings until the outcome of the challenge to the proceedings is known. Similarly, if the outcome of the challenging proceedings is taken on appeal, the execution proceedings will also be suspended pending the outcome of the appeal. Once the appeal is decided the execution proceedings may

---

[1] Dubai Court of Cassation Judgment 235/93 dated 30 January 1994, Dubai Court of Cassation Judgment 541/99 dated 16 April 2000.

[2] Article 244 of the Civil Procedure Law. Supreme Court of Cassation Judgment 448 for the year 20 dated 6 June 2000.

proceed as normal in accordance with any guidelines set out by the Appeal Courts or as requested by the claimant. It may take between 6-12 weeks before judgment is passed in respect of the challenge. The assets which were attached before the objection will remain under attachment until judgment.

Often, a judgment debtor will challenge the execution proceedings simply to delay the execution of the judgment. Challenging the proceedings is also used to delay the enforcement of the judgment as the challenging proceedings automatically suspend the execution process. As such, only the first challenge will suspend the execution of the judgment.[1] A second challenge filed by the same party will not suspend the execution of the judgment. However, a challenge filed by a different party for the first time will suspend the execution, subject to outcome of the challenge proceedings.

Challenge proceedings may take weeks or months before being finalised as it follows the same course as a normal action before the case is reserved for judgment. The appeal process that applies to a normal action will also apply to the objection process.

7.4 Sale by Auction

Should the judgment debtor fail to pay within 15 days of notice being served on him, or upon the finalisation of any challenge, the Execution Court may proceed against the judgment debtor as indicated above. This will include making a new attachment against the assets through the Execution Court or upholding an initial attachment which the judgment creditor may have obtained before the judgment.

Following the attachment, unless payment is received in full, the Execution Court may proceed with the auctioning of the attached assets to satisfy the judgment delivered in favour of the judgment creditor or part thereof.

The auction procedure is rather technical, lengthy and very administrative. It is meant to secure the interests of both the judgment debtor and the judgment creditor. Therefore, it may take months before the assets are auctioned and sold. Given that the judgment debtor or the judgment creditor has the right to object to the price or the procedure of the sale, an auction may be delayed several times before going ahead.[2]

---

[1] Articles 244(4) and 244(5) of the Civil Procedure Law.

[2] Supreme Court of Cassation Judgment 19 for the year 13 dated 16 February 1992.

The attached assets which may be either movable or immovable, shall be auctioned in the following manner:

1. The sale will be carried out by public auction supervised by the Executive Judge, and the successful buyer must pay the price immediately.[1] The auction will not commence until the Clerk of the Execution Court lists all the assets that have been attached and describes the conditions of sale. During the auction process, the Clerk of the Execution Court will also note down any objections and difficulties.
2. The Clerk must post on the door where the attached goods are held and on the court notice boards a notice indicating the day, time and place of the sale together with a list of the items and a general description.[2] The Executive Judge may order that the notice be published in a newspaper with the costs thereof to be deducted from the proceeds of the sale.[3]
3. The name of the bidders, their identity, residence, and place of work will be included with the offer made by each bidder. Once the auction has been finalized, the name of the final bidder, together with the amount for which the assets have been sold must be noted down and put to the Judge for his decision.
4. If the auction is delayed or adjourned, notice of the same must be noted down in the sale minutes.
5. If no one comes forward to buy assets the auction will be extended to the following day or following first working day. If no acceptable bid is put forward for the amount assessed, (and the assets have been assessed by an expert), the auction will be adjourned and an announcement to this effect will be made. After the second auction, the Clerk of the Execution Court will put the matter to the Executive Judge to decide whether to proceed with further auctions or to sell the assets according to the bids put forward even if the same were less than the value assessed. In such a case the Executive Judge will decide either to auction the property for a third or fourth time or as he may deem appropriate or to agree on the sale of the property for an amount lower than the assessed amount of the assets.
6. If the bidder fails to pay the amount immediately or withdraws his bid, the assets will be auctioned in the same way for any amount and the bidder who has first agreed to buy will be compelled to pay the shortfall.[4] However, he will not be entitled to any amount paid if the assets were sold for a higher amount, as this amount is for the benefit of the creditors and the owner of the assets.

---

[1] Article 282, 284 of the Civil Procedure Law.

[2] Article 279(2) of the Civil Procedure Law.

[3] Article 279(3) of the Civil Procedure Law.

[4] Article 284 of the Civil Procedure Law.

7. The Clerk of the Executive Court will stop the bidding on the remaining assets if the amount which was recovered from the sale of some of the assets satisfies the debts and the expenses.[1]
8. If any person is challenging the ownership of the assets which have been sold and attached by the court in connection with some proceeding before the court, such person must file an action before the court to take possession of the assets which he claims to own. If an action is filed before the court by the person who claims the right, he is the right holder and the execution proceedings and the auctioning process will stop subject to the outcome of such action.[2]
9. An action to reclaim the assets or to prove that the assets do not belong to the judgment debtor by any party must be filed against all parties to the action, the execution proceedings or the auction, to enable the claimant to prove that he and not the judgment debtor is the owner of the assets.
10. If the action is dismissed, the execution proceedings and the auction proceedings will resume.
11. Other movable assets such as stocks, bonds, proceeds and shares may also be sold by auction. These assets tend to be in the hands of a third party and will be attached first by way of a garnishee order and then auctioned as described above.[3]

The judgment creditor is advised to monitor the proceedings and where possible even assist the court to find a bidder and to sell for value. The judgment debtor can always stop the sale by auction, even at an advanced stage if he comes forward and settles the judgment debt.

7.4.1 Auctioning Movable Property

The Execution Court, upon the request of the judgment creditor and following the confirmed attachment of the judgment debtor's assets, may proceed with the sale of the assets.

If the asset is cash attached at a bank or other third party there will be no sale, only a request made by the court to the bank or the person holding the money, to transfer the money into court.[4] When the court receives the

---

[1] Article 285 of the Civil Procedure Law.

[2] Article 309 of the Civil Procedure Law. Supreme Court of Cassation Judgment 161 for the year 15 dated 12 June 1994.

[3] Article 290 of the Civil Procedure Law.

[4] Dubai Court of Cassation Judgment 444/98 dated 7 February 1999.

money it will be released to the judgment creditor, less any costs owed to the court or experts appointed by the court.[1]

However, if the attachments are movable property such as machinery, equipment and goods, the court will have to auction it. The auctioning of movable property may proceed in the following manner:

1. If the goods were attached before the action (precautionary attachment), and the judgment creditor has obtained a final judgment, the Clerk of the Execution Court will confirm the attachment by noting this in the minutes of the attachment. He will inspect the goods at the location or as deposited with the custodian. This is the second minute conducted by the Execution Court for the purpose of auctioning the assets, the first minute was made at the time when the goods were attached before the action.
2. If the goods were not attached before the action and the attachments were made after the action through the Execution Court, the Execution Court need not make a further minute. The attachment minute in this case will be used for auctioning the goods.
3. If the goods are difficult to value, an expert will be assigned to value them or if the goods are such that they are difficult to sell without pre-valuation, the court may, at its discretion, appoint an expert to determine the market value of the goods before auctioning the same. This procedure may be followed even after the initial auction should the courts realise that it is difficult to sell the goods without carrying out a valuation. A valuation is usually conducted by an expert drawn from those experts listed at the courts[2] and the judgment creditor will be required to pay for the cost for the expert's services which will be recovered from the auction proceeds at a later date.
4. Once the attachment is made, the Executive Judge will fix the date, hour and place of the sale[3] and the public will be invited to attend. The execution bailiff will then list the goods and post an announcement on the auction board at the courts as well as in a local daily newspaper.[4] The cost of the newspaper advertisement will be paid by the judgment creditor who may recover the cost later from the proceeds of the auction or from the judgment debtor if he has paid the money into court. The list of the goods to be attached is provided and anyone wishing to examine them can do so prior to the auction by making a request to the Executive Judge well in advance of the auction date. Once sanctioned, a date or time will be arranged for viewing the goods in the presence of

---

[1] Articles 316 and 320 of the Civil Procedure Law.

[2] Article 69 of the Law of Evidence.

[3] Article 279 of the Civil Procedure Law.

[4] Article 279 (2) and (3) of the Civil Procedure Law.

the court bailiff. It is unlikely that a detailed examination will be allowed. The Judge may specify a minimum price (especially with valuable goods) and will assess the value with the help of an expert.

5. The auction will take place at the office of the Clerk of the Execution Court, at the court. On the day of the auction, the bidders will submit their offer in writing to the court accompanied by a further commitment to purchase the goods at a certain value. There is no need for the bidder to make any deposit or payment at this stage. The bidder however should be prepared to make a deposit for the full amount or at least a part of it as his offer may be accepted on the same day, although it is unlikely that this will happen. If the court accepts the bid, it is likely that the court will require payment in cash or by certified cheque immediately. In exceptional circumstances, the court may grant the bidder one to two days to make payment in full provided a deposit is paid at the auction.

Following receipt of all bids, the court bailiff will forward the file to the Judge with his recommendations. The Executive Judge will decide on one of the following:[1]

1. To accept the highest bid and to order the bidder to deposit the money in full immediately or within a few days at the court and to take delivery of the goods.
2. To re-auction the goods attached in order to obtain a higher price. At this stage the Judge may or may not set up a minimum value for the bidding.
3. To appoint an expert to value the goods or the equipment, if needed and to adjourn further bidding until the expert has filed his report.
4. Order the re-bidding of the goods through another auction via the same procedure, where another date will be set for auctioning the goods and invite bidders by publication and by further announcements on the courts' board.
5. If another bid is announced or if an expert is appointed, the bidding will be adjourned and none of the bids offered will be regarded as accepted. The bidders will be required to bid again at the second auction scheduled or after the expert has filed his report. The second auction will follow the same process and the Judge may decide on options 1 to 4 listed above a second time. This process may be repeated several times before the Judge decides to accept the highest bid.
6. When the bids close the matter is put to the Judge to make a final decision. It is possible for another bidder to come forward and put a higher bid on the same day or on the following day, i.e. even after the bid has been closed. There is no restriction whatsoever on the Judge to accept the highest bid made on the day of the auction, or to sell the

---

[1] Articles 282, 283 and 284 of the Civil Procedure Law.

attached goods to the bidder who came in subsequently with a higher bid. It is therefore open for bidders to come forward and to increase their bids if, once the Judge has reviewed the file, they come to know the highest bid. They may come forward on the following day or the day after with another offer which will be considered by the Judge provided he has not yet delivered his final order.

7. Once a bid has been accepted, the Judge will ask the successful bidder to pay the money in cash or by a certified cheque immediately. Once the money is paid into court the bidder will receive his goods within two to three days. In special cases such as a vessel which is lying at the port or equipment which requires special care or in respect of which there are fees payable, it is advisable for the bidder to ensure that there will be no other attachments, costs or other problems involved which may delay the release of the goods to him even after payment into court. In some instances where a vessel has been arrested by another court in the UAE or where there is an outstanding port charge, the release of the vessel may be delayed until the port charges are cleared and other attachments vacated. It is also possible that the release of the equipment and the goods may be delayed if the judgment debtor filing a challenging application challenges the sale of the goods or the value of the same in court. Such a challenge may result in a delay with the release of the goods to the bidder unless the Judge decides otherwise.

8. It is not possible for a bidder to withdraw his bid once he has submitted it and deposited the money, although it is possible to withdraw from the bid prior to depositing the money. In certain circumstances, the bidder may have difficulty in taking delivery of the goods or have other complications relating to the goods, and the Judge may release the money to the bidder or hold the money until the goods are sold through another auction. In other words the Judge will re-auction the goods and if sold to another bidder the first bidder may get his money back from the court and withdraw his bid. Such an application and procedure is entirely at the Judge's discretion and be dependent on the circumstances. The court may, however, deduct the difference in price from the first bidder if the goods are subsequently sold for a lower price.[1]

9. Once the movable property has been sold by auction it will be free of any encumbrances, mortgage or any other claim whatsoever. Any party who has an interest in the movable property by way of an attachment, mortgage or otherwise before the goods were sold by auction will only have an interest in the proceeds of the sale but not in the movable property itself. The title in the movable property will pass to the buyer who has bid for it through the court. While this is the position in the UAE, it may not have a bearing on a legal jurisdiction outside the UAE. This does not necessarily include any rental charges or government

---

[1] Article 304 (4) of the Civil Procedure Law.

charges for servicing or securing the goods.
10. Any objection, grievance or challenge to the sale procedure or the distribution of the proceeds of sale amongst the creditors must be filed with the Executive Judge as detailed above.
11. If the movable property remains unsold even after several auctions for the value assessed by the court or by the expert appointed by the court, the court may reduce the value. This is usually done by an application to the Executive Judge. This is why the judgment creditor needs to be active in the process.
12. The sale of goods by auction does not limit the court's power to give an order for attachment against other assets owned by the judgment debtor especially if the movable property to be auctioned does not satisfy the full amount claimed.
13. The Execution Department at the court will supervise all the procedures and will deliver an official minute in respect of the movable property to the successful bidder once the money has been deposited into court and the Judge has authorised the sale.
14. If transfer of the title of the property requires a letter to be written to a particular department to affect the transfer from the judgment debtor to the bidder, then the court may write to the relevant department instructing them to do so.
15. If the judgment is delivered in one court but the actual attachments against the goods (whether before action or after the execution has taken place) are in another court within the UAE, then by way of petition the actual auction and subsequent delivery of the movable property to the bidder will be carried out by the court where the assets are physically located with the close co-operation of the court which delivered judgment. The final proceeds of the sale are subject to any distribution of money that may need to be distributed by the court where the assets are located, following which the balance will be transferred to the court which has jurisdiction on the substance of the matter.[1]

The judgment debtor, members of the judiciary or of the public prosecution, execution agents, agents of the Clerk of the Court or public prosecution and legal representatives of the judgment debtor, are not permitted to bid at an auction by themselves or by someone acting on their behalf.[2]

---

[1] Articles 220(4) and 221 of the Civil Procedure Law

[2] Article 312 of the Civil Procedure Law.

7.4.2 Auctioning Immovable Property [1]

The procedure relating to the auction of immovable property, the challenging procedure and the delivery of the property is similar to that of movable property including the appointment of an expert (who must be appointed)[2], with some differences:

1. Proceedings commence when the judgment creditor files an application with the Executive Judge, to attach the land. This application must contain the name, title, profession, domicile and place of work of the judgment creditor and judgment debtor and a description of the land. The application must be accompanied by a copy of the judgment and a copy of the notice or evidence that the judgment debtor has been given notice to pay and he has failed to pay despite such notice. A copy of the title deed of the property must also accompany the application and if the details are not provided, the judgment creditor may petition the court[3] for an order enabling the Clerk of the Court to enter the premises and record the relevant details and the description of the property or to write to the Lands Department and request further information about the property.
2. Once the Executive Judge is satisfied that the documents are in order, he will issue an order to attach the property and order the court bailiff to attend the Lands Department or write an official letter to the Lands Department to attach the property and note the same in their records.[4] The court bailiff shall obtain official evidence of any other rights registered on the property if any.
3. The Clerk of the Court shall inform the judgment debtor, the possessor of the property and the guarantor of the attachments, of the attachment order by letter[5] within seven days of the judgment. He will also inform any other creditors registered with the court, who will immediately become a party to the attachments.
4. Before proceeding with the sale of the land, the Executive Judge will notify the judgment debtor to pay the amount due within one month from the date of such notice failing which the court will proceed with the sale of the real estate property by auction.[6] The judgment debtor may request the adjournment of the sale of the property. The Executive Judge will only adjourn the sale for a further period in one of the following circumstances:

---

[1] Article 292 of the Civil Procedure Law.
[2] Article 295(3) of the Civil Procedure Law.
[3] Article 292(2) of the Civil Procedure Law.
[4] Article 293(1) of the Civil Procedure Law.
[5] Article 294 of the Civil Procedure Law.
[6] Article 295(1) of the Civil Procedure Law.

a) If the income of the land for a period of three years is adequate to pay for the debt, interest and the court fees. In such a case the Judge will assign the debt to the creditors and collect the rent directly until final payment. However, if the creditors are unable to collect the rent or the process is obstructed, the Judge will proceed with the sale.

b) If the income of the land for a period of three years will not satisfy payment of the debt, interest and the fees but the judgment debtor has other income which, with the rents will satisfy payment of the debt within three years and it becomes evident to the Judge that selling the property will cause the judgment debtor great hardship, the Judge may defer the sale of the property. If the judgment debtor defaults, the Executive Judge will proceed with the sale on the application of the judgment creditor.

5. If the judgment debtor fails to pay within the notice period, nor submits an application for adjournment within the notice period, the Executive Judge will fix a date, time and place for the sale by auction.[1]

6. Before announcing the sale, the Executive Judge **must** appoint an expert to value the real estate property, and to file a report within 30 days from the date on which he was appointed.[2]

7. The Clerk of the Court will, 30 days prior to the sale, inform all parties (including the judgment debtor, possessor, mortgagor or guarantor) of the date, time and place of sale. A notice will also be published in two daily newspapers, a copy shall be placed on the court notice board and a copy shall be placed in a prominent place at the property concerned.[3] The notice itself shall contain the following information:[4]

   a) The name, title, vocation, domicile, place of work of the judgment creditor, judgment debtor, possessor, mortgagor or guarantor,
   b) A description of the immovable property which forms the basis of the claim,
   c) Conditions of sale, basic price as valued by the expert, expenses and deposit required by the prospective purchaser (provided it is not less than 20% of the price),
   d) The court concerned and the date, time and place of the auction.

8. It is possible for the claimant to obtain an order from the Executive Judge to publish a notice of the sale through a different source to publicise the auction, but this shall not delay the sale.[5]

---

[1] Article 295(2) of the Civil Procedure Law.

[2] Article 295(3) of the Civil Procedure Law.

[3] Article 295(4) of the Civil Procedure Law.

[4] Article 296(1) of the Civil Procedure Law.

[5] Article 296(2) of the Civil Procedure Law

9. If the immovable property is divisible, each part of the real estate property can be sold separately and independently. If a part of the immovable property is sufficient to satisfy the debt, the Judge will proceed in selling such part before proceeding with the sale of the other parts by auction.[1] Furthermore, if there is more than one property attached and auctioned for sale, each one of them will be sold independently unless the Judge, after obtaining the opinion of an expert finds that it is better for the property to be sold in one auction as one unit to one bidder.
10. Real estate property can only be auctioned and sold to a UAE national taking into consideration the procedure for transfer of real estate property. It may however be possible nowadays to sell property in certain locations to GCC nationals. In Dubai, it may be possible for certain properties to be sold to non-UAE nationals depending on the nature and location of the land.
11. The judgment creditor will benefit from any income earned from the property after the attachment order, which earnings will be deposited with the court. If the property is not rented the judgment debtor will be considered as the custodian to safeguard the interests of the creditors until the property is sold. He will also be considered a custodian for the income from the date on which he was given notice of the attachments.
12. If the property is mortgaged, or is possessed by another party or any person who has an interest in the property, notice to the mortgagor or the person who has an interest in the property must be given before attaching the property and before auctioning the same. Any court order for the sale or transfer of property will be invalid for the judgment creditor and other creditors if the sale took place after the attachment has been ordered to include any mortgage or transaction that has been transacted on the property.
13. Any party who has an interest in the property may file an objection to the validity of the notice, or of the procedure regarding the auction, but must do so at least 3 days prior to the auction date.[2] This must be a formal application to the Executive Judge in charge of the auction. The Judge will then decide whether to proceed with the auction or to delay the same on the grounds of objection.
14. The Executive Judge may order the judgment creditor to deposit an amount into court before proceeding with the auction to cover the auction costs. This amount will be deducted from the proceeds of the sale and the judgment creditor will be reimbursed for it.[3]
15. The auction will be conducted by the Executive Judge on the day, time and place fixed for the sale. The Executive Judge will accept the highest price provided that it is not less than the base price recommended by the

---

[1] Article 297 of the Civil Procedure Law.

[2] Article 301(1) of the Civil Procedure Law.

[3] Article 302 of the Civil Procedure Law.

expert. If the bid is less than the price recommended by the expert or if no bidders come forward, the auction may be delayed to the following day. If no bidders came forward for the base price, the auction will be delayed for the third day less 5% of the base price and thereafter everyday where the price will be less 5% until the value is reduced by 25%. If no bidder comes forward at this stage, the sale will be adjourned for a period of three months. At this auction (after three months) the property will be sold for any price.[1]

16. The successful bidder must deposit the full purchase price plus expenses into court within 10 days following the bid. Once he deposits the full amount within this period the Executive Judge will confirm that the sale is final.[2] In practice, the ten days may be exceeded.
17. Should the successful bidder fail to make payment, the Judge will then offer the property to the second bidder for an amount put forward. He must furnish the amount within 10 days. Should the second bidder refuse, the Executive Judge must put the land up for re-auction within 15 days in accordance with the procedure outlined above.[3]
18. Any person who is not prohibited to bid may increase the bidding price, even if the bid has been closed, within the 10 days period following the bid, provided that it is not less than 10% more than the bidding price. In such a case the bidder must deposit the amount into court immediately as soon as the Judge confirms the bid has been successful. In such a case the Judge will re-open the bid to re-auction the property within seven days. If no other bidders bid for a higher price, the property will be sold to the higher bidder.[4]
19. The successful bidder who fails to pay for the property will be liable to pay the difference in price if the property was sold for a lesser value in the second bid. If however the bid was for a higher price he will not be entitled to the difference between his bid and the higher price. This will be paid to the creditors or the owner of the property as the case may be.[5]
20. The bidder may provide the court with a certified cheque or a bank guarantee. If he was also a creditor and not prohibited from buying the property he may also bid for the property and set-off the price against the debt.[6]
21. If, for reasons beyond his control, it is not possible for the purchaser to effect the sale and registration of transfer within 30 days from the date of the award of the bid, he may withdraw his bid without any liability.

---

[1] Article 303(2) of the Civil Procedure Law.

[2] Article 304(1) of the Civil Procedure Law.

[3] Article 304(2) of the Civil Procedure Law.

[4] Article 304(3) of the Civil Procedure Law.

[5] Article 304(4) of the Civil Procedure Law.

[6] Article 304(5) of the Civil Procedure Law.

If the Judge approves the withdrawal, the auction must take place again in the same procedure referred to above.[1]
22. The judgment debtor may, at any time even after completion of the bidding and before registration of transfer of the property in the name of the bidder with the Lands Department, pay the full amount into court and take back his property.[2]
23. If the auction did not proceed due to legal reasons or because the judgment creditor did not follow it up, it must be repeated within 15 days. If, however the auction is left for a period of six months and no action was taken, the entire process must start afresh.[3]
24. The closing of a bid will be in the same form as a judgment, binding on all parties and will be enforced by law against all parties.[4] The decision to close the bid is not subject to an appeal unless there has been a defect in the announcement or the auction process. An appeal must be filed within seven days from the date of the judgment.[5]
25. The Judge will order the Lands Department to register the property in the name of the successful bidder according to their procedure and registration of the property will clear the property from any debts, liability or claim from a third party whatsoever.[6]
26. Any person who challenges the sale or claims that he has a right over the property or wishes to annul the process must file an action before the court to annul the procedure or the sale. If an action is filed the same process will be suspended pending a final judgment.[7]

As mentioned above, the sale of immovable property is a technical and slow process and requires intensive follow up. The court usually tends to proceed with the sale of immovable property as a last resort and the judgment debtor may be given several opportunities to pay before the property is sold. It is clear that because of the above technical procedure, it is possible to file several challenges and to appeal against the procedure to the Court of Appeal to delay the sale.

The matter also becomes complicated when there is a mortgage registered on the property in favour of a bank or other financial institution or third party who is not a party to the action, as this may cause further delays in the sale of the property and the release of the mortgage at the Lands Department.

---

[1] Article 304(7) of the Civil Procedure Law.

[2] Article 304(8) of the Civil Procedure Law.

[3] Article 305 of the Civil Procedure Law.

[4] Article 306 of the Civil Procedure Law.

[5] Article 307 of the Civil Procedure Law.

[6] Article 308 of the Civil Procedure Law.

[7] Article 309 of the Civil Procedure Law.

The judgment debtor can always cancel the sale even after a bid has been accepted or the money paid into court if he comes forward and pays the adjudged amount in full. The payment of the judgment debt in full by the judgment debtor will reverse the process before the title is actually transferred into the name of the bidder. If the title has been transferred and the bid was finalised by the Judge the case is considered closed.

7.5   Distribution of Sale Proceeds

When the attachment has been levied on cash or an attached property is sold, the execution proceeds will be divided amongst the attaching creditors.[1] The Executive Judge and the Execution Department at the courts will carry out distribution of the sale proceeds.

If the proceeds are sufficient to settle all the attachments, the court will order that each creditor will receive his payment. If, however, there have been other precautionary attachments in cases which have not been adjudicated by the court or any other court and the attachment has been confirmed, the proceeds of sale or part of it will be held by the court to satisfy those attachments until that case is determined. The only exception is that of preferent claims which will have to be paid, especially if the debt in the attachment case is not a preferent claim. In other words, if there are cases which have not yet been determined and enjoy an attachment over the same property which has been sold, the proceeds of sale will be held by the court to satisfy the attachment in cases which have not been judged with the exception of preferent claims which have to be paid immediately unless the debt in the attachment case is also a preferent claim.

Therefore, it is important that the party who has an attachment and also enjoys a preferent claim closely monitors the distribution of the proceeds from the sale to ensure the application is considered at the time when the money is available for distribution amongst the creditors. If no supervision is carried out by the judgment creditor to ensure that the application is heard during the distribution of the sale proceeds, it is possible that the debt may not be considered as preferent and the money may be distributed to other preferent creditors. However, if there is an attachment, the debt will always be considered as a concurrent debt when the time comes to distribute the proceeds of the sale.

The distribution of the proceeds of sale is made on a preferent basis. Normally, a preferent claim has to be submitted by the judgment creditor.

---

[1] Article 316 of the Civil Procedure Law.

With the exception of government debts (which the court itself will consider as preferent), the courts rarely consider a debt as preferent unless notified of such debt by the judgment creditor requesting an order for a preferent claim.

Preferent claims are not normally decided upon by the court that hears the substance of the matter. The court, when giving judgment may refer to the preferent claim or deal with it as it is dealing with the merits of the case, but generally a preferent claim is considered to be within the jurisdiction of the Executive Judge. It is for the Execution Court to decide what determines a debt as preferent at the time of distributing the proceeds.[1] This will only be considered following judgment on the merits and at the stage of the execution. Therefore, even if the judgment on the merits does not classify the debt as preferent, the Executive Judge will normally have jurisdiction to decide on whether a particular debt is a preferent or not.[2]

7.5.1 Order of Distribution[3]

Generally the Execution Courts will distribute the proceeds of sale in the following order:

1. Normally the courts pay out government debts out of the proceeds of the sale before any other creditor. A government debt includes a judgment confirming that the amount claimed is owed to the government for charges or services including ports authority fees, customs duty or any other charges owed to the government pursuant to a law, decree or ordinance or any other regulations that are implemented by the Federal government or the local government in the UAE. The court normally pays out if the government has a final judgment delivered in its favour and have joined other creditors in attaching the assets or after the proceeds of sale are deposited into court. This may vary from one Emirate to another and the courts may pay government debts based on a written claim. Some courts in the UAE will pay out to the government out of the proceeds of the sale and treat their claim as a priority debt such as port charges and other confirmed services without the need for a judgment unless the amount is disputed and cannot be verified by the court.
2. Alimony (maintenance) ranks second in priority and will be paid out of the proceeds of sale provided that the claimant has a final judgment

---

[1] Article 319 and 320 of the Civil Procedure Law.

[2] Dubai Court of Cassation Judgment 70/99 dated 1 May 1999, Supreme Court of Cassation Judgment 494 for the year 19 dated 2 February 1999.

[3] Supreme Court of Cassation Judgment 154 for the year 16 dated 3 January 1995.

confirming that the amount is due and payable as alimony by order of the court.

3. Wages and employee benefits outstanding against an employer where the attached assets consist partly of the employer's assets. This will include wages for crewmembers of a ship. An employee who has a final judgment will recover wages and benefits as a priority debt after the government claims and alimony. Labour claims are defined under the UAE Labour law No. 8 of 1980.

4. There are specific priority debts created by statute or decree, which rank after the above but before any other creditors. Examples (not ranking) of such are as follows:

   a) Fees payable to a custodian who was appointed by the court as a custodian for attached assets will have the privilege of legal expenses.[1]
   b) An employee has a priority right over his employer's assets to cover the employee's dues from the employer.
   c) Lawyer's fees are a priority claim to recover the fees payable for legal proceedings, however, such priority right will be in conjunction with the money received and awarded in a case where the lawyer has outstanding fees.[2]
   d) Maritime debts in accordance with Article 84 of the Maritime Code.[3]
   e) Legal expenses and judicial expenses of the court.
   f) The landlord's right against a tenant's furniture as security for the payment of the rent.

5. A mortgagee who has a confirmed and valid mortgage over a property by possession or registration as provided by the law. A mortgagee who has a mortgage on immovable property or a charge over a movable property will rank fifth after all the above creditors and before any other normal creditors when it comes to distribution of the proceeds of sale of assets which are either mortgaged or pledged to the judgment creditor. If the mortgage is held to be invalid the mortgagee will then rank on the same level as all other creditors. In order to determine whether the mortgage is valid, the relevant mortgage and real estate property law of the Emirate concerned must be considered. With regard to movable property, the relevant articles of the UAE Commercial Transactions Code[4] and the Civil Procedure Law must be considered. Should the mortgage or charge be valid, the mortgagee will receive payment or the balance of the payment after the above creditors have been paid. If there

---

[1] Article 275 of the Civil Procedure Law.

[2] Supreme Court of Cassation Judgment 494 for the year 19 dated 2 February 1999.

[3] UAE Federal Law No. 26 of 1981. Dubai Court of Cassation Judgment 70/99 dated 1 May 1999.

[4] UAE Federal Law No. 18 of 1993.

is more than one mortgagee he will be treated with priority as provided by the law or by agreement.
6. The balance of the proceeds will then be distributed amongst the remaining creditors on a pro rata basis. If there is no money remaining from the proceeds to distribute then the creditors will attempt to locate other assets belonging to the judgment debtor to execute against.

In order to be entitled to a preferent claim under any of the categories mentioned above, the creditor concerned must proceed to the Execution Court with an application claiming preference supported by evidence to substantiate such a claim. The court will not consider a debt as preferent even if the judgment creditor has a judgment and an attachment over the assets or the proceeds of sale unless a formal application is made to the Execution Court claiming preference. Any decision made by the court will be subject to an appeal to the Court of Appeal.

It is also possible for any party who has an interest in the matter to interfere in such an application and request the court to reject the other party's application for preference or to dismiss it and consider their application as preferent before that of the other application. Challenging an application for preference by creditors who have no priority claim or by a mortgagee against statutory priority is rather common and often heard before the court. If an application is challenged, a formal hearing date will be set by the court where both parties will be invited to make their submissions supported by their evidence to the courts. After a few hearings the court will reserve the case for judgment and decide whether the challenging party's application should be considered as a preferent claim or not. The court may also decide whether to distribute the proceeds or how to distribute them. Any judgment delivered by the court will be subject to an appeal.

If the court decides that the debt is a preferent claim, the money will be distributed as indicated by the judgment even if an appeal is filed, although, practically, if an appeal is filed immediately, depending on the court, it may delay the release of the money because the files are sent to the court of Appeal as soon as an appeal is filed. However, legally, a judgment creditor who has obtained a judgment confirming his preferent claim may be able to receive payment immediately from the court as decided by the Judge. If the Court of Appeal refers the decision back to the Court of First Instance or amends it, the matter will then be returned to the Executive Judge for a decision on the matter according to the guidelines set out by the Court of Appeal.

It is not unusual for the Judge at the Execution Court, while proceeding with the execution proceedings and the distribution of the proceeds of sale, to hear several applications challenging the distribution of the money before the money is finally distributed amongst all the creditors. It is also possible that the file may go back and forth to the Appeal Court several times due to appeals filed by one of the judgment creditors or the judgment debtor himself challenging a decision made by the Executive Judge.

It is therefore important that the judgment creditor who has a preferent claim or a mortgage over the property not only to monitor his own case but also to monitor the cases of other creditors to ensure that any decision delivered on another case does not prejudice his rights. If there is a risk that his rights may be affected by another application he may file an application to interfere in the other application and to put his arguments to the Judge for consideration.

7.6 Destruction of goods by the Execution Court

One of the remedies available to the court is the confiscation and destruction of goods. If the court order provides for the destruction of goods such as those which have been attached in connection with trademark or copyright claims, or the confiscation of the goods, the Execution Court will carry out the destruction and the confiscation.

If the goods have already been attached before the action, the Execution Department will proceed with the confiscation of the goods following the execution notice and the destruction of the same as ordered by the court. If the goods are of the special nature, i.e. health products or chemical products, the court may seek the expertise of government departments such as the Health Department or the Environmental Department at the relevant municipality to assist in the destruction. Destruction will be carried out privately by the court bailiff and on some occasions (dependant upon the court), a representative of the claimant and the defendant will be invited to attend. Details of the destruction with photographs are recorded in a file.

If goods are confiscated they become government property and will be disposed of by the court according to the court's own procedure. On some occasions if the confiscated goods are good for human consumption the court will distribute them to charity.

7.7 Conclusion of the Execution Procedure

The execution procedure will not end until the final payment is made for the full amount claimed. Therefore, until payment is made in full, the execution file will remain open and the claimant may make further applications to request attachment of the judgment debtor's assets or search for other assets. An execution order may not be implemented if it is left for a period of 15 years from the date of the last application by the claimant or if it is left for a period of 15 years from the date of the order without being implemented.[1] The court will also continue to keep the execution current subject to a final payment or an application from the judgment creditor confirming that he has received the full amount from the judgment debtor and requesting the court to close the file.

However, if the judgment creditor and the judgment debtor reach a settlement whereby they have scheduled the payments or made an arrangement that payments be made in a certain way following attachments or otherwise, they may make an application to the Judge to make the settlement agreement an order of court. Accordingly, the attachment of the assets may not be fully lifted though the execution proceedings have been suspended or cancelled, as this will be subject to the settlement agreement. It is possible that the settlement agreement will provide that the attachments will be enforced by the court subject to payment of the final installment or upon a particular date that the parties have agreed on in their settlement agreement. The court will uphold such an agreement and the attachments will remain in force until the judgment debtor pays the amount in full or receives confirmation from the judgment creditor requesting the court to close the execution file.

If the judgment debtor defaults on the payment or the settlement, the judgment creditor may initiate the execution procedure by making a simple application to court. No notice will be served on the judgment debtor unless the court otherwise believes it would be appropriate to do so before proceeding with any further action.

---

[1] Article 225(4) of the Civil Procedure Law.

7.8 Imprisonment for Failure to Pay

A person may be imprisoned if he fails to pay the amount set out in the judgment against him.[1] However, the judgment creditor must provide the court with evidence that the judgment debtor is incapable of paying and that he has not paid despite notice to do so.[2]

The Executive Judge may, upon the request of the judgment creditor, order the judgment debtor to be confined if the judgment debtor refrains from making payment in accordance with an execution order relating to a final payment order despite being able to settle such debt, or if there is a fear that the judgment debtor may abscond from the country. The judgment debtor shall not be considered as being capable of paying if his ability to pay is entirely based upon assets which may not be attached or sold. If he is incapable of paying, no order for imprisonment will be made. The duty rests on the judgment creditor to show evidence that the judgment debtor is capable of paying.

A judgment debtor shall be considered sound and capable of making payment and the Executive Judge shall order his imprisonment in any of the following circumstances:[3]

1. If the judgment debtor smuggles or conceals his assets for the purpose of harming the creditor and due to such action it has become impossible for the judgment creditor to execute against such assets.
2. If the debt is payable under an installment plan, or if the debtor was one of those who guaranteed payment before the court or the Executive Judge unless the debtor proves new circumstances have occurred after the decision of installments was passed or after making the guarantee affecting its soundness and rendering it incapable of payment of installments or any part thereof.
3. If the amount of the judgment is a legally decided alimony.

The Executive Judge shall, in the cases detailed in the two preceding paragraphs, order the confinement of the debtor for a period not exceeding one month which may be renewed for further periods. If the debtor has a permanent and stable place of residence, he may not be confined for more than six consecutive months. Renewal of the debtor's confinement may be ordered after the lapse of 90 days from his release if he continues to refrain

---

[1] Article 324 of the Civil Procedure Law.

[2] Dubai Court of Cassation Judgment 23/94 dated 28 May 1994, Supreme Court of Cassation Judgment 524 for the year 19 dated 28 September 1999.

[3] Article 324(2) of the Civil Procedure Law.

from paying the execution amount despite being capable to settle the debt, provided the total period of the debtor's confinement does not exceed 36 months in total regardless of the number of debts or creditors.

The Executive Judge must hear the debtor's deposition every time he orders the renewal of the debtor's confinement or if the creditor so requests. The debtor shall be detained in a separate place away from those detained or adjudged in criminal cases and the prison management shall enable the debtor to use the available means of communication with the outer world in order to be able to manage his affairs for the settlement of the debt or enter into agreement with his creditors.

The execution of a confinement order shall not lead to the abatement of the right for which confinement was ordered and does not preclude mandatory execution in legally decided manners.

Imprisonment may not be ordered in the following circumstances:[1]

1. If the judgment debtor is not yet eighteen years old or is more than seventy years old.
2. If the judgment debtor has a child who is not yet 15 years old and his spouse is dead or imprisoned for any reason.
3. If the judgment debtor is the creditor's spouse or ancestor and the debt is not a decided alimony.
4. If the judgment debtor has produced a bank guarantee or has introduced a sound guarantor acceptable to the Executive Judge for the settlement of the debt on the due date or if the judgment debtor has disclosed attachable assets in the state which are sufficient to settle the debt.
5. If the debtor is a pregnant woman, the Executive Judge may postpone her imprisonment until one year after delivery to enable her to look after the infant.
6. If it is substantively proven that the debtor suffers from a chronic incurable disease due to which he cannot stand imprisonment.
7. If it is proven that the debtor suffers from a temporary sickness due to which he cannot stand imprisonment, the Executive Judge may decide to postpone his imprisonment until he is well again.
8. If the debt against which execution was ordered is less than AED 1,000 unless it is a financial penalty or decided alimony.
9. If it is clearly evident that the debtor is totally insolvent and has no assets or any other means to pay.

---

[1] Article 326 of the Civil Procedure Law.

7.9 Execution in Criminal Matters

The Execution Department at the court does not carry out execution in criminal matters as the Execution Department is only concerned with civil matters. The prosecutor's office is in charge of executing criminal judgments whether it is for a fine or an imprisonment. Therefore, once the court hands down the judgment, the file will be immediately transferred to the execution department at the prosecutor's office to implement the judgment. The prosecutor's office may appeal against the judgment or part of it, or execute the judgment.

Normally, judgments delivered by the Court of First Instance are subject to immediate execution by the prosecutor's office for imprisonment unless the Court of Appeal suspends the sentence and grant bail.

The prosecutor's office is in charge of the execution and such an execution will be carried out independently at the prosecutor's office without the claimant's involvement. If, however, the judgment has a civil aspect where a claimant is awarded the payment of money, he may make an application to the prosecutor's office to release any money that has been deposited with the prosecutor's office in order to satisfy the judgment delivered in his favour. The police force usually assists the prosecutor's office in enforcing the judgment delivered by the court.

The prosecutor's office is not only in charge of enforcing a judgment by imprisonment or fine but also in charge of enforcing a judgment delivered for bail or release from prison. The prosecutor's office will also immediately enforce a judgment delivered in favour of a person found innocent by releasing him or refunding the fine if a fine has been collected.

If a person is sentenced for a year or more in prison, the year is usually calculated as nine months and any time that the accused spends in custody at the police department or the prosecutor's office will be taken into consideration when calculating the time he has served.[1] In other words any time he has served will be credited to him when calculating the time he has served in prison as ordered by the court. If the person is ordered to pay a fine with no imprisonment, should he have spent time in prison, each day that he has served in prison will be calculated at the equivalent for AED 100 per day. However, there will be no refund payable if the time spent in prison exceeds the amount of the fine.

---

[1] This reduced sentence will apply for inmates who have good behaviour. The timing may also vary from one Emirate to another.

Visitation is allowed on specified dates and at specified times at the prison and at the police stations unless visitation is restricted. Normally, visitors are not restricted unless the matter involved is a highly complicated crime and even in such instances, restrictions are limited to the period of the investigation, after which visitation restrictions will be lifted and normal visitation rights allowed. Special visitation rights can be applied for at the prosecutor's office for special needs or for attorney/client confidentiality, if needed, or for special occasions where there is justified reasons for special visitation rights at a time and date specified outside the scheduled visits.

Chapter Eight

APPEAL

8.1 Preliminary Procedure

There is an automatic right for each party, whether a claimant or defendant in an action, to file an appeal against a judgment.[1] Only final judgments can be the subject of an appeal to the Court of Appeal. Interlocutory judgments or judgments on procedure or regarding the calling of witnesses cannot be the subject of an appeal. However, judgments on urgent applications, precautionary attachment orders or objections on jurisdictional points may be the subject of an appeal.[2]

A memorandum of appeal must be filed within 30 days from the date on which the judgment was delivered and in an *ex parte* judgment, within 30 days from the date on which the judgment was served on the respondent. In urgent matters the period is 10 days.[3] The days are calculated from the day following the day in which the judgment was delivered in the presence of the parties or from the day following the day upon which the judgment was served on the respondent.[4]

On appeal, the whole matter will normally be reconsidered by the Court of Appeal no matter what the grounds of appeal may be. Appeals to the Court of Appeal may be filed on points of law and fact and new facts, evidence and arguments may be submitted.[5] It is open to either party to make further

---

[1] Article 158 of the Civil Procedure Law.

[2] Article 151 of the Civil Procedure Law. Supreme Court of Cassation Judgment 21 for the year 17 dated 12 November 1995, Dubai Court of Cassation Judgment 101/95 dated 17 December 1995, Dubai Court of Cassation Judgment 251/95 dated 21 July 1996.

[3] Article 159 of the Civil Procedure Law.

[4] Article 152 of the Civil Procedure Law. Dubai Court of Cassation Judgment 326/97 dated 1 March 1998, Dubai Court of Cassation Judgment 87/99 dated 8 May 1999.

[5] Article 165(2) of the Civil Procedure Law.

arguments, to add to the grounds of appeal, to make further submissions and call for witnesses. Three Judges form the appeal bench, the procedure is similar to that of the Court of First Instance[1] and judgment is delivered by majority.[2]

The appellant will submit written arguments together with supporting documents from time to time and the respondent may request an extension of time in order to comment on the submissions made. Either party to the action may file documents, other evidence, has the right to call witnesses, and the same rules of procedure will be applicable.[3]

The law does not require the appellant to set out all of his grounds of appeal in the original memorandum of appeal, i.e. It is possible for a "holding" appeal be filed without any grounds. In this instance, the appellant may file a detailed memorandum of appeal setting out the grounds of appeal at the first hearing date of the case before the Court of Appeal. It is also possible for further grounds to be added in a supplementary memorandum of appeal or other memoranda or in documents that may be filed by the appellants. Although the law states that the memorandum of appeal must be filed at the first hearing,[4] the courts have been lax in applying this and there are no ramifications for not doing so. It has been held that the grounds of appeal may be filed in general terms and supplemented later.

8.1.1 Notice of Appeal

An appeal must be filed by the appellant or his authorised attorney with the Clerk of the Court at the Court of Appeal.[5] On receipt of the memorandum of appeal (or holding memorandum of appeal), signed by the appellant or his attorney, the Clerk of the Court will open a file for the matter, enter it into the register and allocate an appeal number. The memorandum shall indicate the appealed judgment and its date, the grounds of appeal (unless it is a holding appeal), the remedy sought and information concerning the

---

[1] Article 168 of the Civil Procedure Law.

[2] Supreme Court of Cassation Judgment 612 for the year 20 dated 3 October 2000.

[3] Dubai Court of Cassation Judgment 325/2001 dated 18 November 2001.

[4] Article 162(3) of the Civil Procedure Law. Dubai Court of Cassation Judgment 319 and 327/93 dated 13 February 1994, Dubai Court of Cassation Judgment 100/94 dated 26 November 1994, Supreme Court of Cassation Judgment 255 for the year 15 dated 25 December 1995.

[5] Article 162 of the Civil Procedure Law.

litigants such as names, capacities and domicile.[1] Copies sufficient for the number of parties involved should be submitted.

Following payment of the Appeal Court fees by the appellant, the appeal will be officially registered and a hearing date will be scheduled for the case. The Clerk of the Court will then notify the appellant of the date of the hearing of the appeal and shall prepare the summons to be served on the respondent. The respondent must be notified of the appeal in person at his domicile or his place of work.[2]

Normally, the date of the first hearing of the appeal will be scheduled at the Court of Appeal three to four weeks from the date on which the appeal was filed and the respondent normally will be summoned approximately two weeks from the date on which the appeal was filed.

The Clerk of the Appeal Court has no jurisdiction to examine the appeal whether on its merits or its form neither do they have the right to challenge whether the appeal has been filed within the specified period or not. They will file the appeal irrespective of any grounds at any time it is filed and irrespective of the remedy requested in the memorandum of appeal.

The respondent may file a counter-appeal.[3] If a counter-appeal is filed by the respondent, the counter-appeal will be allocated a separate number, a new file will be opened and following the payment of the court fees, the same hearing dates will be given for the counter-appeal. The Clerk of the Appeal Court will prepare the summons for the counter-appeal and serve notice of the hearing on the respondent advising him of the counter-appeal. Again, there is no need to file a detailed memorandum of appeal in the counter-appeal and a "holding" memorandum of appeal may be filed.

Both files will thereafter be joined and put before the same court to be heard jointly. On the first hearing date of the case, the court will confirm the joining of the two appeals and declare that they will be heard together as they relate to the same subject matter.

---

[1] Article 162(1) of the Civil Procedure Law.

[2] Article 155 of the Civil Procedure Law. Supreme Court of Cassation Judgment 285 for the year 19 dated 20 December 1998.

[3] Article 164 of the Civil Procedure Law. Dubai Court of Cassation Judgment 403/97 dated 21 February 1998, Dubai Court of Cassation Judgment 454/99 dated 29 April 2000, Supreme Court of Cassation Judgment 216 for the year 21 dated 20 February 2001.

8.2 Appeal Proceedings

In both an appeal and a counter-appeal the court will consider legal and factual arguments and may decide to call and hear witnesses or refer the matter to the experts at the Court of First Instance, as the case may be. The Court of Appeal is a court of fact and law and will review the matter in the same way as the Court of First Instance.[1] It will not, however, be permissible to ask for further remedies than those that were put before the Court of First Instance in the Court of Appeal.[2] The court will be limited to those remedies which were requested in the Statement of Claim filed at the Court of First Instance.

The court will consider whether the appeal has been filed within the time period and if not, the appeal may be rejected on its form. The court will also consider whether the matter may be appealed to the Court of Appeal.

8.3 Matters not subject to Appeal

8.3.1 Court of Appeal

There are certain matters that are not subject to appeal at the Court of Appeal. They are as follows:

1. An action which is less than AED 3,000.[3]
2. Certain decisions of the Execution Court apart from those set out in Article 222 of the Civil Procedure Law.[4]
3. The award made by an arbitrator in an arbitration case.[5]
4. The decision made to assess the fees payable to an expert in a case where the expert has filed a report.[6]
5. A decision which has been decided by the court while the case is being litigated,[7] but which did not finally determine the matter according to the meaning of Article 151 of the Civil Procedure Law (i.e. decision

---

[1] Dubai Court of Cassation Judgment 325/2001 dated 18 November 2001.

[2] Article 165(3) of the Civil Procedure Law. Supreme Court of Cassation Judgment 406 for the year 19 dated 23 March 1999.

[3] Article 30 of the Civil Procedure Law.

[4] Dubai Court of Cassation Judgment 317/97 dated 28 February 1998.

[5] Supreme Court of Cassation Judgment 219 for the year 11 dated 10 June 1990.

[6] Supreme Court of Cassation Judgment 159 for the year 20 dated 5 March 2000.

[7] Supreme Court of Cassation Judgment 82 for the year 19 dated 31 March 1998.

made to refer the matter to an expert or to call on witnesses or to join two cases in one file).[1]
6. A decision made by the court in a civil matter ordering one of the parties to pay a fine for misbehaving or being in contempt of court.

8.3.2 Court of Cassation

There are certain matters that are not subject to an appeal to the Court of Cassation. These are as follows:

1. A decision made by the Court of Appeal where the claim does not exceed AED 10,000.[2]
2. Decisions made by the Court of Appeal in connection with the execution procedure where the Court of Appeal were reviewing the judgment of the Court of First Instance or an appeal relating to execution procedure. It is however possible to appeal the decision of the Court of Appeal in an execution matter but not an execution procedure.[3]
3. An appeal filed against the judgment not delivered from the Court of Appeal, as it is not possible to appeal a Court of First Instance judgment to the Court of Cassation directly.

8.4 Appeal prior to Final Judgment

It is possible in limited circumstances to appeal against a judgment delivered by the Court of First Instance while the court is still hearing the matter if a full and final decision has been made on an issue.[4] The following decisions will be subject to an appeal to the Court of Appeal even if the Court of First Instance has not yet determined the subject matter of the proceedings by final judgment:

1. A decision made by the court in connection with a dispute where the court has decided that it has or does not have jurisdiction in respect of the subject matter whether on the grounds of local jurisdiction or arbitration. In such a case, the judgment delivered by the Court of First

---

[1] Dubai Court of Cassation Judgment 327/2000 dated 11 November 2000.

[2] Supreme Court of Cassation Judgment 86 for the year 17 dated 3 July 1995, Dubai Court of Cassation Judgment 25/97 dated 11 October 1997, Dubai Court of Cassation Judgment 397/99 dated 6 February 2000.

[3] Dubai Court of Cassation Judgment 545/99 dated 29 April 2000.

[4] Article 151 of the Civil Procedure Law.

Instance will be subject to an appeal to the Court of Appeal and further to the Court of Cassation.[1]

2. While there is an issue or dispute over a matter and the court has determined this matter by a final judgment i.e. where the court has decided to liquidate a company or to dissolve a company and continue the process by referring the matter to a liquidator or to an expert to resolve the case. In such a case the judgment delivered by the court is the determination of a final issue, which can be appealed to the Court of Appeal and further to the Court of Cassation.[2]
3. A judgment dealing with an objection against an execution procedure or an execution matter and an attachment against the assets in connection with the execution procedure. However, execution procedures can only be appealed to the Court of Appeal where execution matters can be appealed further to the Court of Cassation.[3]
4. An appeal against a decision where the court decided to halt the process of the case because of a defence filed by the party and where the other party does not wish the process to stop. In such case an appeal may be filed to the Court of Appeal and further to the Court of Cassation.

If an appeal is filed in any of the above matters the court will hear the arguments and submissions of both parties in the normal course or rule that the issue may not be contested until after final judgment.

8.5 Appeal after Final Judgment

However, with regard to the merits of the case, following the submission of both parties' arguments, documents, experts' reports or documents requested by the court, the court will reserve the case for judgment. The judgment will be delivered in an open hearing on a date set by the court. The court may adjourn the case for judgment only once and must thereafter reserve it for judgment.[4]

---

[1] Supreme Court of Cassation Judgment 227 for the year 17 dated 28 January 1996, Supreme Court of Cassation Judgment 316 for the year 18 dated 30 September 1997.

[2] Supreme Court of Cassation Judgment 62 for the year 15 dated 29 June 1993, Dubai Court of Cassation Judgment 202/96 dated 7 July 1997.

[3] Supreme Court of Cassation Judgment 328 for the year 14 dated 15 June 1993, Supreme Court of Cassation Judgment 258 for the year 18 dated 19 November 1996, Dubai Court of Cassation Judgment 435/97 dated 26 April 1998.

[4] Article 127 of the Civil Procedure Law.

Any judgment delivered by the Court of Appeal will be subject to further appeal to the Court of Cassation. Appeal to the Court of Cassation must take place within 30 days from the date on which the judgment was delivered if the party was present at the hearing or within 30 days from the date on which the party was served with full details of the judgment and the grounds.[1] If the parties were not present at the hearing in which the judgment was delivered or if they were not informed of the grounds of the judgment and the reasoning of the Court of Appeal, the period for appeal will remain open[2] for either party until they are fully and officially served with the grounds of the judgment, thus the 30-day period only commences from the date of notification.

8.5.1 Counter-Appeal and Sub-Appeal

It is open for either party to file a counter-appeal independently from the appeal filed by the other party against the judgment.[3] A counter-appeal must be filed within the 30-day period, failing which the court will reject it in its form.

However, besides the option of filing a counter-appeal, either party may file a sub-appeal even if the 30-day period has lapsed.[4] This is a new procedure which was introduced by the Civil Procedure Law in 1992 which allows either party who has not filed an appeal within the 30-day period to file a sub-appeal if the other party to the action has appealed against the judgment within the 30-day period. The sub-appeal will be treated as a counter-appeal even though it is filed after the 30-day period. The appellant in the sub-appeal will have all the benefits and rights of a counter-appeal and may make submissions as in a normal counter-appeal. The only exceptions and differences are as follows:

1. The sub-appeal may only be filed and be admissible before the court if there has been an appeal filed by the other party with the Court of Appeal within the 30-day period. In other words, if the other party appealed within the time period, the sub-appeal will be allowed and be

---

[1] Article 176 of the Civil Procedure Law. Supreme Court of Cassation Judgment 506 for the year 20 dated 24 October 1999, Supreme Court of Cassation Judgment 349 and145 for the year 20 dated 26 November 2000.

[2] Supreme Court of Cassation Judgment 87 for the year 18 dated 22 December 1996.

[3] Article 164 of the Civil Procedure Law.

[4] Article 164(2) of the Civil Procedure Law, Dubai Court of Cassation Judgment 454/99 dated 29 April 2000.

joined with the appeal. If the other party files no appeal there will be no sub-appeal.
2. The sub-appeal must be filed with the court before or on the date of the first hearing scheduled for the case and not after.[1] The sub-appeal will only be admissible in its form and will only be successful in its form if filed by formal application and provided that the memorandum is filed on or before the first hearing date of the original appeal filed by the other party.[2]
3. The sub-appeal is not independent from the main appeal filed by the other party. Thus, if the original appeal has been filed after the lapse of the 30-day time period or being dismissed in its form, the sub-appeal will be dismissed in its form as well.
4. The sub-appeal will only succeed as long as the main appeal continues to be heard by the courts. Therefore if the appellant in the original appeal decides to withdraw his appeal, the sub-appeal will be withdrawn automatically with the main appeal, as it cannot exist without it.[3]
5. The merits of the sub-appeal may succeed irrespective of the outcome of the main appeal. As far as the merits are concerned, the main appeal may be dismissed on its merits but the sub-appeal may succeed on its merits, as it will be treated independently from the main appeal when it comes to its merits.[4]

Either the main appellant or the sub-appellant may appeal to the Court of Cassation against a judgment delivered by the Court of Appeal. The sub-appellant, once the judgment of appeal is delivered may appeal independently to the Court of Cassation. The appeal and the judgment delivered in connection therewith will be considered independently, as is the case of a counter-appeal. The Court of Appeal is independent from the Court of First Instance and the judgment delivered by the Court of Appeal will be binding on the lower court and the Execution Court as far as the merits of the case are concerned.

---

[1] Whether that hearing is within the 30 day period or after the 30 day period.

[2] Supreme Court of Cassation Judgment 216 for the year 21 dated 20 February 2001.

[3] Article 164(3) of the Civil Procedure Law. Dubai Court of Cassation Judgment 420/94 dated 15 August 1995.

[4] Dubai Court of Cassation Judgment 127/97 dated 11 May 1997.

8.5.2 Decisions of the Court of Appeal

The Court of Appeal in most cases will decide on the following:

1. If a Court of First Instance judgment was dismissed for lack of jurisdiction of the court and the Court of Appeal reverses the judgment and finds that the UAE court has jurisdiction, the matter will be referred back to the Court of First Instance to hear the matter since the Court of Appeal has decided that the court has jurisdiction.[1]
2. If the Court of First Instance does not look into the merits of the case and has dismissed the case in its form or for a technical reason and the Court of Appeal has reversed its decision, it must refer the matter back to the Court of First Instance. It cannot hear the merits of the case until the Court of First Instance has exhausted its power to look at the merits.[2]
3. If the Court of Appeal decides to reverse the judgment delivered by the Court of First Instance in part or whole it will hear the matter and deliver a judgment on the merits reversing the Court of First Instance's decision in part or whole.[3] Normally, the courts will not refer the matter back to the Court of First Instance to re-hear the case and amend the judgment. The Court of Appeal will decide on the merits on its own accord and determine the matter. The judgment however will be enforceable at the Court of First Instance, at the Execution Court immediately following judgment. If the court decides to uphold the judgment delivered by the Court of First Instance, the court will uphold the judgment and dismiss the appeal.
4. On rare occasions, the Court of Appeal may uphold the judgment delivered by the Court of First Instance but amend the reasoning given by the Court of First Instance if it is not correct in law.
5. The Court of Appeal on very rare occasions may refer the matter back to the Court of First Instance for a decision if the Court of Appeal is of the opinion that by dealing with the matter itself, the Court of Appeal may prejudice the party's right to have the case heard by the Court of First Instance and on appeal. If the Court of Appeal is of the view that the party would benefit from having their case heard at two instances, that they were not being given the right to do so and that therefore the party would lose their right of having the case heard in two instances, the Court of Appeal may refer the matter back to the Court of First

---

[1] Article 166 of the Civil Procedure Law. Supreme Court of Cassation Judgment 39 for the year 21 dated 20 December 2000.

[2] Supreme Court of Cassation Judgment 75 for the year 19 dated 1 January 1999.

[3] Supreme Court of Cassation Judgment 141 for the year 15 dated 27 March 1994, Dubai Court of Cassation Judgment 40/95 dated 25 June 1995, Supreme Court of Cassation Judgment 239 for the year 16 dated 25 September 1995, Dubai Court of Cassation Judgment 325/2001 dated 18 November 2001.

Instance. For example, if the Court of First Instance heard the case and served the summons on one of the parties or the summons was null and void and an appeal has been filed and court found in favour of the appellant, the Court of Appeal will refer the matter back to the Court of First Instance to avoid the appellant not being given the chance to defend himself at the Court of First Instance and thereafter at the Court of Appeal.[1]

All the above decisions (even in the case where the matter is referred back to the Court of First Instance) will be subject to an appeal to the Court of Cassation within a 30-day period, the only exception being in respect of a judgment delivered by the Court of Appeal in execution procedural matters. Appeal on execution procedural matters will not be subject to an appeal to the Court of Cassation. If an appeal is filed to the Court of Appeal in an execution procedural matter in connection with a judgment delivered by the Execution Court, the Court of Appeal judgment will be final there will be no further appeal to the Court of Cassation.[2]

8.6 Appeal to the Court of Cassation

Federal judgments delivered by the Federal courts (Abu Dhabi, Sharjah, Fujairah, Ajman and Umm Al Quwain) are subject to an appeal to the Federal Supreme Court of Cassation in Abu Dhabi. Judgments delivered by the Dubai Court of Appeal are subject to an appeal to the Dubai Court of Cassation. There is no Court of Cassation in Ras Al Khaimah. The UAE Federal Supreme Court of Cassation in Abu Dhabi is also the Constitutional court.

An appeal to the Court of Cassation, whether before the Dubai Court of Cassation or the Supreme Court of Cassation of the Federal court, must be filed by a duly licensed advocate. An appeal filed by the appellant to the Court of Appeal without a licensed advocate will be dismissed in its form.[3]

Not all lawyers are licensed to practice before the Court of Cassation, lawyers who have five or more years of experience are permitted to appear

---

[1] Supreme Court of Cassation Judgment 64 for the year 21 dated 7 November 2000.

[2] Article 173(2) of the Civil Procedure Law. Dubai Court of Cassation Judgment 265/97 dated 16 November 1997.

[3] Article 177(1) of the Civil Procedure Law. Dubai Court of Cassation Judgment 329/97 dated 8 November 1997.

before the Court of Cassation, provided that they have been officially licensed separately under the Federal system.[1]

The Court of Cassation is formed by five Judges and judgment is usually delivered by majority. An appeal to the Court of Cassation is rather technical and the specific procedure must be followed failing which the appeal will be dismissed in its form.[2] Unlike an appeal to the Court of Appeal, appeal to the Court of Cassation may be dismissed on technicalities on more than one ground. Care should be taken to comply with the formalities, failing which the appeal may be dismissed. The following technical issues must be carefully considered when filing an appeal to the Court of Cassation:

1. The appellant must file his appeal against the judgment delivered by the Court of Appeal within 30 days from the day following the day on which the judgment was officially served on him or from the date on which the judgment became known to him.[3]
2. A period of 10 days is added to this 30 day time period if the appellant is domiciled outside the jurisdiction of the court and 60 days if the appellant is domiciled outside the UAE.[4]
3. The amount involved in the subject matter or the appeal to the Court of Cassation must exceed AED 10,000 or be unlimited in cases where the amount involved in the case is undetermined. Appeal for cases for less than AED 10,000 will not be admissible to the Court of Cassation, and it is not based upon the amount that the Court of Appeal has awarded a party but the value of the original claim.[5]
4. The application must be signed by an advocate licensed and registered with the Court of Cassation[6] and accompanied by a receipt indicating

---

[1] Supreme Court of Cassation Judgment 205 for the year 20 dated 5 March 2000, Supreme Court of Cassation Judgment 145 and 349 for the year 20 dated 26 November 2000.

[2] Article 177(4) of the Civil Procedure Law. Supreme Court of Cassation Judgment 60 for the year 18 dated 11 June 1996, Supreme Court of Cassation Judgment 474 for the year dated 21 January 1997, Dubai Court of Cassation Judgment 156/99 dated 20 June 1999.

[3] Article 176 of the Civil Procedure Law. Supreme Court of Cassation Judgment 619 for the year 18 dated 22 November 1998, Supreme Court of Cassation Judgment 93 for the year 19 dated 14 November 1999.

[4] Article 12 of the Civil Procedure Law. Dubai Court of Cassation Judgment 60/2000 dated 11 June 2000.

[5] Article 173(1) of the Civil Procedure Law. Dubai Court of Cassation Judgment 25/97 dated 11 October 1997, Supreme Court of Cassation 97 for the year 21 dated 1 November 2000.

[6] Supreme Court of Cassation Judgment 129 for the year 21 dated 6 December 2000.

that the court fees have been paid,[1] a copy for each of the litigants and the Clerk of the Court and the Power of Attorney of the lawyer representing the appellant.

5. The application must indicate the judgment in terms of which the appeal has been filed and refer to the date of the judgment, the reference number, the court from which the judgment was delivered and any other details to identify the judgment.[2] In the Supreme Court of Cassation, the lawyer is, in addition to filing a copy of the Power of Attorney, also required to provide evidence that the signatory of the Power of Attorney had the necessary capacity.

6. The application must indicate the names and capacities of the respondents, their representatives and details of the addresses to which the summons should be served.[3]

7. The application must set out the decision made by the Court of Appeal and the legal grounds of appeal.[4] The legal grounds should not refer to a memorandum or submissions made to the Court of First Instance or Appeal. The grounds of appeal must be specific, relying on particular legal grounds and attacking the judgment delivered by the Court of Appeal on a particular legal argument that must be set out clearly to the Court of Cassation.[5] Unlike the position in the Court of Appeal, a "holding" appeal is not admissible to the Court of Cassation and an appeal framed in this manner is likely to be rejected if it contains no legal grounds for appeal.

8. Appeals on merits or facts are not admissible to the Court of Cassation, only legal arguments and appeals on matters of law are admissible. The appeal should focus only on legal arguments which may not have been dealt by the court or the law which has been wrongfully interpreted or applied by the Court of Appeal.[6] The Court of Cassation will not review the decision of the Court of Appeal on the merits or understanding of the facts of the case even if the Court of Appeal wrongfully understood the facts of the case, unless their understanding of the facts of the case were based on a wrong understanding of a legal argument or a particular law which the Court of Appeal wrongfully applied to the case. The Court of Cassation will not interfere in the Court of Appeal's ability to assess and determine the facts of the case.

---

[1] Article 177 of the Civil Procedure Law. Supreme Court of Cassation Judgment 322 for the year 14 dated 16 March 1993.

[2] Supreme Court of Cassation Judgment 32 for the year 16 dated 21 June 1994.

[3] Supreme Court of Cassation Judgment 364 for the year 18 dated 31 December 1996.

[4] Supreme Court of Cassation Judgment 86 for the year 18 dated 28 May 1996.

[5] Supreme Court of Cassation Judgment 410 for the year 17 dated 19 March 1996.

[6] Dubai Court of Cassation Judgment 14/98 dated 10 May 1998, Supreme Court of Cassation Judgment 208 for the year 19 dated 19 May 1998, Dubai Court of Cassation Judgment 53/2000 dated 20 May 2000.

9. The appeal must be filed by the party who has lost the appeal not by the party in whose favour judgment was granted.[1] In addition, the appeal must be filed against a party to the case in the Court of Appeal.[2] No new party may be introduced into the Court of Cassation if they were not originally a party at the Court of Appeal.[3]
10. As indicated above, an appeal relating to execution procedure is not admissible to the Court of Cassation.[4]
11. The appeal to the Court of Cassation must be based entirely on the judgment delivered by the Court of Appeal and not of that delivered by the Court of First Instance.[5] The Court of Cassation will not review or consider the judgment delivered by the Court of First Instance and therefore the grounds of appeal should not deal with the judgment delivered by the Court of First Instance and should concentrate only on the judgment delivered by the Court of Appeal.[6]
12. It is not possible to call witnesses, experts or to file any further documents[7] before the Court of Cassation as all these submissions will not be entertained by the Court of Cassation. Therefore, emphasis should be placed on the legal argument rather than making special submissions to the Court of Cassation to hear witnesses or to appoint an expert. The court may, however, of its own accord order a party to file documents or exhibit evidence in limited circumstances.[8]

8.6.1 Notice

After receiving the memorandum of appeal filed by the appellant, the Clerk of the Court of the Court of Cassation will serve the same on the respondent within 10 days of the registration of the appeal.[9] The same summons procedure applicable before the Court of First Instance will be applicable before the Court of Cassation.

---

[1] Dubai Court of Cassation Judgment 190/95 dated 20 October 1996, Supreme Court of Cassation Judgment 355 for the year 17 dated 31 December 1996, Supreme Court of Cassation Judgment 472 and 491 for the year 19 dated 29 June 1999.

[2] Supreme Court of Cassation Judgment 292 for the year 17 dated 30 January 1996.

[3] Dubai Court of Cassation Judgment 286/95 dated 30 March 1996.

[4] Article 173(2) of the Civil Procedure Law. Dubai Court of Cassation Judgment 548/99 dated 29 April 2000.

[5] Supreme Court of Cassation Judgment 264 and 346 for the year 20 dated 24 May 2000.

[6] Supreme Court of Cassation Judgment 284 for the year 16 dated 3 January 1995.

[7] Supreme Court of Cassation Judgment 607 for the year 20 dated 18 October 2000.

[8] Supreme Court of Cassation Judgment 231 for the year 10 dated 18 April 1989.

[9] Article 180 of the Civil Procedure Law.

After the service of the summons has been affected on the respondent, he will be given 15 days to respond to the appeal.[1] The Clerk of the Court in the meantime will request the judgment file from the Clerk of the Court at the Court of Appeal. No hearing date will be scheduled and the submission of the response will be made to the Clerk of the Court of the Court of Cassation in writing. No supporting documents are permissible whether in the memorandum of appeal or in the submissions made by the party in response to the appeal. The court will ignore any supporting document filed.

It will then take several weeks and sometimes months before the Court of Cassation will set a hearing date to hear both parties' arguments orally before the court. At the hearing, the court may decide either to adjourn the case or to summon one of the parties who has not been summoned properly, or following the hearing of both parties' arguments, to decide to reserve the case for judgment. Neither party will be allowed to make further submissions and often the Court of Cassation will reserve the matter for judgment at the first hearing date of the case.

It is possible before the Supreme Court of Cassation in Abu Dhabi that no hearing date will be scheduled at all. Following the receipt of the respondent's submissions the court may take a few weeks or few months to review the file and then deliver judgment and serve same on the parties without a hearing.

8.6.2 Application to Suspend the Execution of Judgment

An appeal to the Court of Cassation will not normally prevent the enforcement or execution of a final judgment delivered by the Court of Appeal.[2] The judgment of the Court of Appeal is considered to be a final judgment and good for execution. As such, execution will not be suspended by the fact that the appeal is filed with the Court of Cassation unless the appeal relates to the ownership or vacation of immovable property.

However, in certain instances, it is possible to apply to the Court of Cassation to suspend the execution of the judgment subject to the outcome of the appeal to the Court of Cassation. The Court of Cassation may suspend the enforcement of a final judgment delivered by the Court of Appeal until the Court of Cassation has had an opportunity to study the file

---

[1] Article 180(3) of the Civil Procedure Law.

[2] Article 175 of the Civil Procedure Law.

and deliver judgment. In such cases, the Court of Cassation usually orders the judgment debtor to file a bank guarantee as security for the judgment.[1]

The appellant may request the Court of Cassation to suspend the judgment delivered by the Court of Appeal and to order that no execution should proceed until the judgment of Court of Cassation is determined. This request is made in the same application of appeal filed by the appellant to the Court of Cassation, or in a separate application to be filed with the memorandum of appeal. The appellant will be required to state the grounds upon which he believes that execution against him may irrevocably alter his circumstances or to indicate that he has good grounds upon which to win the case at the Court of Cassation and that therefore execution should be suspended until the Court of Cassation determines the appeal.

The Court of Cassation, before reviewing the merits of the appeal will ask the other respondent to respond to the application to suspend the execution of the judgment and will schedule a hearing date to hear both parties' arguments. After hearing both parties arguments at a hearing (which is usually scheduled on an urgent basis), the court will issue judgment on the same day whether to suspend the execution of the judgment or to reject the application to suspend the execution.

Pending the hearing by the Court of Cassation, the Execution Court will proceed with the execution of the judgment delivered by the Court of Appeal irrespective of whether there has been an application filed with the Court of Cassation to suspend the judgment of the Court of Appeal or not. The Execution Court will only suspend the judgment if there has been a formal decision made by the Court of Cassation to suspend the execution or in the case of a dispute relating to immovable property (real estate property)[2] after evidence is provided that an appeal to the Court of Cassation has been filed.

In the majority of cases, the Court of Cassation will reject an application filed to suspend the execution of a judgment unless the Court of Cassation is shown that there exists good grounds that the application should be entertained and an order be granted to suspend the execution. Accordingly, suspending the execution of the judgment is only granted in rare occasions and only in circumstances where the court believes that the execution can wait, or there is a risk that the circumstances, if changed, cannot be corrected if the judgment is reversed or that the Court of Appeal erred in applying the law, or that in all likelihood the appellant will win his appeal

---

[1] Article 175(2) of the Civil Procedure Law.

[2] Article 175(1) of the Civil Procedure Law.

and the judgment will therefore be changed. However, in disputes relating to real estate or a decision relating to eviction in rental disputes, execution will be automatically suspended.

If the Court of Cassation grants the request and makes an order to suspend the execution, the execution will be suspended and no further execution proceedings will resume until the final judgment is delivered by the Court of Cassation on the merits of the appeal. Suspension of the execution will have no bearing whatsoever on the merits of the appeal. If the judgment is reversed, the execution will continue to hold until another final judgment is delivered on the matter. However, if the appeal to the Court of Cassation is dismissed the execution will proceed in the normal manner.

A separate nominal fee must be paid to the Court of Cassation on filing an application to suspend the execution of the Court of Appeal. If the Court of Cassation finds in favour of the appellants, it will decide on suspension of the execution of the judgment. A brief judgment will have no grounds subject to the outcome of the appeal. The court may set out conditions to suspend the execution. On some occasions the court may order the judgment debtor to provide a bank guarantee for the amount judged as security before the Court of Cassation or the Execution Courts before the order can be suspended. If the bank guarantee is not filed the order will not be suspended.[1]

The Court of Cassation may also suspend the order in whole or in part and decide to proceed with the remaining parts.[2]

8.6.3   Judgment of the Court of Cassation

Normally, the Court of Cassation does not determine the matter. If the Court of Cassation finds in favour of the appellants, it will cancel the judgment delivered by the Court of Appeal in whole or in part and refer the matter back to the Court of Appeal to correct the judgment. Therefore, the judgment of the Court of Appeal or part of it may be cancelled and have no legal value and any execution proceedings which have resumed based on the judgment of the Court of Appeal or part thereof and which have been cancelled by the Court of Cassation will be cancelled and reversed.

---

[1] Article 175(2) of the Civil Procedure Law.
[2] Article 185 of the Civil Procedure Law.

If there has been an attachment by the Execution Court or any action taken by the Execution Court based on the judgment delivered by the Court of Appeal which has been cancelled by the Court of Cassation, such attachment or action will be cancelled and reversed. Therefore, if the judgment of the Court of Appeal is reversed by the Court of Cassation in full, it will be considered as if it was never delivered. However, if the judgment of the Court of Cassation reverses only part of the Court of Appeal judgment, the execution proceedings relating to that part will be cancelled and the valid part of the Court of Appeal judgment will continue to be valid and may be executed.[1]

Once a matter has been reversed and referred back to the Court of Appeal, the Court of Appeal will allocate a hearing date where both parties will be invited to attend before the court as in a normal appeal case.

Both parties will then be allowed to make written submissions and to file further evidence and request permission to call witnesses. The court, upon the request of one of the parties or at its own discretion, may refer the matter to an expert to review and decide on one or two issues in the case. It is the task of the Court of Appeal to evaluate the facts, consider the matter and review new facts and evidence and to make a decision at its discretion. Any decision made by the Court of Appeal or a judgment rendered may not contradict the principles set out by the Court of Cassation in its judgment.[2] In other words the Court of Appeal can still find in favour of the claimant or the defendant irrespective of the findings in the judgment provided that the judgment of the Court of Appeal does not contravene the legal grounds which were set out by the Court of Cassation when the matter was referred back to the Court of Appeal.

Accordingly, the appellant cannot always take it for granted that the Court of Appeal will find in his favour nor that he will have the judgment reversed by the Court of Cassation as the Court of Appeal may find in favour of the respondent based on the different grounds and facts. Therefore, the case will have to be argued and adequate evidence submitted to the Court of Appeal when the matter is referred back to the Court of Appeal.

---

[1] Article 185(2) of the Civil Procedure Law.

[2] Article 184 of the Civil Procedure Law. Dubai Court of Cassation Judgment 297/95 dated 17 March 1996, Dubai Court of Cassation Judgment 332/96 dated 9 March 1997, Dubai Court of Cassation Judgment 353/2000 dated 21 January 2001, Supreme Court of Cassation Judgment 383 for the year 20 dated 13 March 2001.

The second judgment delivered by the Court of Appeal will also be subject to an appeal to the Court of Cassation. The same conditions, time frames and procedures will be applicable to the second appeal. The second appeal to the Court of Cassation will be considered to be a new appeal and may be based on a similar grounds to that of the first appeal or on new grounds as decided by the Court of Cassation. However, the appeal to the Court of Cassation must be based on the legal grounds of the second judgment delivered by the Court of Appeal. The judgment of the Court of Appeal will be good for execution immediately unless suspended or reversed by the Court of Cassation in a normal procedure for filing an appeal to the Court of Cassation. The second appeal to the Court of Cassation will be treated in the same manner as the first appeal.

However, if the Court of Cassation decides to reverse the judgment delivered by the Court of Appeal in whole or in part, the Court of Cassation in this second appeal will not refer the matter back to the Court of Appeal except in a very exceptional circumstances. In the second appeal, the Court of Cassation will deal with the appeal itself and deliver a final judgment on the matter correcting the judgment of the Court of Appeal if the Court of Cassation finds in favour of the appellants. In such a case the judgment delivered by the Court of Cassation will be the final judgment on the matter and will substitute the Court of Appeal judgment in whole or in part.

The Court of Cassation will, however, not refer a matter back to the Court of Appeal to correct a judgment if the appeal is based on the following grounds:

1. If the appeal relates to a jurisdiction matter, the Court of Cassation will determine the matter without having to refer the matter back to the Court of Appeal even if the appeal was filed for the first time before the Court of Cassation.
2. If the appeal relates to a labour matter (which are usually dealt with on an urgent basis) and should it involve a simple and straightforward issue, it may be dealt with by the Court of Cassation directly without having to refer the matter to the Court of Appeal. This is to avoid having to delay the matter by referring the matter back to the Court of Appeal and at its discretion, the Court of Cassation may decide on the merits of the case and deliver a final judgment without referring the matter back to the Court of Appeal.
3. Matters relating to the enforcement of an arbitration award and challenging the authority of the arbitrator, or any other matter relating to arbitration, the Court of Cassation may decide on the matter without referring the matter back to the Court of Appeal.

4. On family issues relating to inheritance, custody, maintenance and in urgent family cases the Court of Cassation may decide on the matter without referring it back to the Court of Appeal.
5. The Court of Cassation may decide that the action is ready and suitable for judgment, and that there is no need to refer the matter back to the Court of Appeal.
6. If the matter is on appeal a second time with the Court of Cassation and the Court of Cassation has already made a decision on the matter and referred the matter to the Court of Appeal to deal with, the Court of Cassation will not to refer the matter back to the Court of Appeal a second time and deliver a final judgment.

Judgments delivered by the Court of Cassation are final and are not subject to any further appeals to any other court.[1] The Court of Cassation judgment is not subject to a review or challenge.[2] The guidelines set out in the judgment delivered by the Court of Cassation must be followed by the Court of Appeal if the matter is referred back to the Court of Appeal and those issues decided upon by the Court of Cassation in the judgment must be adhered to.

8.7 Review of Judgments

Final judgments cannot normally be reviewed, challenged or reconsidered. The judgment will be final even if it becomes evident in the future that the judgment was wrong, and it will not be subject to any consideration regardless of the situation and no matter how harsh the judgment may have been.

However, the Civil Procedure Law has introduced a new procedure for reviewing a final judgment if it becomes evident that the judgment was obtained by misleading the court, by cheating or on the basis of forged documents. This is an exception to the rule that a judgment is final and it is only applied in very restrictive and exceptional cases. Even if such grounds

---

[1] Article 187 of the Civil Procedure Law.

[2] Supreme Court of Cassation Judgment 5 for the year 22 dated 12 January 1997, Supreme Court of Cassation Judgment 179 for the year 17 dated 8 April 1997, Dubai Court of Cassation Judgment 7/96 dated 11 May 1997, Supreme Court of Cassation Judgment 5 for the year 21 dated 29 March 1998, Supreme Court of Cassation judgment 6 for the year 25 dated 31 March 1998, Supreme Court of Cassation Judgment 4 for the year 21 dated 17 November 1998.

are evident in the case, the law provides that only in the following exceptional circumstances may the judgment be reviewed:[1]

1. If a fraud is committed by either party which has affected the judgment.
2. If the judgment was based on papers which, after the issue of the judgment were admitted or adjudged to be forged or if the judgment was based on the testimony of a witness which was later established to be false.[2]
3. If, after the verdict, the appellant obtained documentation which he was prevented by the other party from obtaining and which is conclusive to the case.
4. If the decision was made by the court in favour of the claimant for something more than what he has asked for or beyond the remedy that he has requested.
5. If there is a decision that contradicts the substance of the judgment or there was a contradiction between the substance and the conclusion.[3]
6. If judgment was enforceable against a party who was not actually a party to the action or joined in the proceedings provided that such person proves that the person who represented him cheated or committed a fraud.
7. That the decision was made when the party (whether a person or an entity) was not properly represented in the proceedings.

A review application must be filed with the court which delivered the final judgment and cannot be filed by a way of appeal. For instance, an application to review the judgment of the Court of First Instance must be made to the Court of First Instance. If the complaint relates to a judgment of the Court of Appeal, the application must be made to the Court of Appeal and not to the Court of Cassation. If the judgment to be reviewed is that of the Court of Cassation, the application to review must be made to the Court of Cassation. In other words, review of a judgment must be made to the court which has made the final judgment and not to the Appeal Court by way of an appeal.

---

[1] Article 187 referring to Article 169 of the Civil Procedure Law. Dubai Court of Cassation Judgment 6/96 dated 3 May 1997, Dubai Court of Cassation Judgment 2/2001 dated 5 January 2002.

[2] Dubai Court of Cassation Judgment 64/2000 dated 24 December 2000, Dubai Court of Cassation Judgment 40/2001 dated 5 May 2001.

[3] Dubai Court of Cassation Judgment 59/94 dated 10 July 1994, Supreme Court of Cassation Judgment 320 for the year 17 dated 12 December 1995, Dubai Court of Cassation Judgment 171/95 dated 1 June 1996, Dubai Court of Cassation Judgment 275/97 dated 20 December 1997, Dubai Court of Cassation Judgment 7/99 dated 8 May 1999.

To date, as far as the author is aware there has been no decision by any court to review any judgment delivered by the court. All applications made for review have been rejected as they have not satisfied the strict grounds set out by the law which grounds are being applied very strictly and conservatively by the courts. Since this process is not clear under the law, unless the evidence is strong and conclusive it is unlikely that an order will be delivered for the review of a final judgment.

Chapter Nine

ARBITRATION

9.1 Introduction

While arbitration is becoming a popular form of dispute resolution in the UAE, the UAE does not have an arbitration law, save for a limited number of provisions within the Civil Procedure Law (see below under 9.2). Apart from specific regulations relating to disputes arising out of dealings in securities and commodities in the Dubai Financial Market and the Abu Dhabi Securities Market,[1] there has not been any serious attempt to introduce an independent arbitration law under any model in the UAE.

Although arbitration in the UAE is still in its infancy, there are two arbitration centers located in the Emirates of Abu Dhabi and Dubai respectively. In 1993, the Abu Dhabi Chamber of Commerce and Industry established an arbitration center called the Abu Dhabi Commercial Conciliation and Arbitration Center to settle commercial disputes through conciliation or arbitration.[2] The Center introduced procedural rules and a schedule of costs for conducting an arbitration in the UAE. These rules deal with local and international arbitration and arbitration cases have already been conducted under these rules.

In Dubai, the Dubai Chamber of Commerce and Industry established the Dubai Chamber of Commerce and Industry Commercial Conciliation and Arbitration Center[3] in 1994. The Center supervises domestic and international arbitration under the Dubai Chamber of Commerce and Industry Rules of Commercial Conciliation and Arbitration of 1994. In

---

[1] The Arbitration Regulations No. 1 for the year 2001 were passed pursuant to the Stocks and Commodities Law No. 4 of 2000 providing that a dispute arising out of dealings in securities and commodities whether in the Dubai Financial Market or the Abu Dhabi Securities Market must be determined by arbitration. The regulations set out the procedural requirements for such arbitration.

[2] See http://www.adcci.gov.ae

[3] See http://www.dcci.gov.ae

addition to these Rules, the Center provides a schedule of costs. Both the Abu Dhabi and Dubai Centers for Commercial Conciliation and Arbitration have panels of arbitrators who are specialists in their respective fields.

An arbitration award in the UAE can be delivered by a Muslim or Non-Muslim, national or non-national and there is no restriction on the nationality or the religion of the arbitrators or the place of arbitration other than what is mentioned in 9.9 below concerning the difficulties in enforcing foreign arbitration awards. There is also no restriction on the subject of the arbitration other than it may not be possible to arbitrate matters relating to labour and commercial agency.

The UAE has not formally acceded to the New York Convention on the Recognition and Enforcement of Foreign Arbitral Awards (10 June 1958) and therefore there are no international rules governing the enforcement of foreign arbitration awards in the UAE other than the local law and procedure which is applicable to the enforcement of foreign judgments generally.[1] However, in May 2003 the UAE Cabinet of Ministers approved a suggestion made by the Minister of Justice to accede to the New York Convention. The matter has now been put to the Supreme Council of the UAE for ratification, which is expected shortly. This will have a major effect on the enforcement of foreign arbitration awards in the UAE and is also likely to influence changes to the UAE arbitration law generally.

The UAE has ratified the GCC treaties for the enforcement of judgments delivered by the GCC courts and arbitration awards delivered by the GCC countries[2] and has entered into bilateral agreements with France[3] and India.[4] The UAE has also entered into certain co-operative arrangements with other countries.[5]

---

[1] Articles 235 to 246 of the Civil Procedure Law.

[2] The Riyadh Convention ratified by the UAE on 15 April 1999, by Federal Decree No. 53 of 1999.

[3] The Judicial Co-operation and Recognition of Judgments in Civil and Commercial Matters between the UAE and the Republic of France, ratified by the UAE on 27 April 1992 by Federal Decree No.31 of 1992.

[4] Agreement between the UAE and the Republic of India on Juridical and Judicial Co-operation in Civil and Commercial Matters for the Service of Summons, Judicial Documents, Judicial Commissions, execution of Judgments and Arbitral Awards, ratified by the UAE on 29 March 2000 by Federal Decree No. 33 of 2000.

[5] See Appendix 2.

In spite of this, while an arbitration clause is normally upheld by the UAE courts, enforcement of awards especially foreign, may entail pitfalls, the most important of which are dealt with below.

9.2   Formalities

Legislation concerning arbitration is currently confined to Articles 203 to 218 of the Civil Procedure Law which provide rules governing arbitration, the enforceability of the arbitration clause, the validity of the arbitration award, the appointment of arbitrators and some relevant procedures in the arbitration process in a relatively simple manner.

For the arbitration clause to be upheld it must be in writing.[1] There must be a clear indication that the parties have agreed to submit any dispute arising out of an agreement to arbitration. Evidence must be provided that the party has knowledge of the arbitration clause which is normally implied when a party has signed an agreement, for the arbitration clause to be valid.[2] Accordingly, the court may not uphold an arbitration clause which is printed as a standard clause in fine print as general terms and conditions or at the back of an invoice or a delivery note. However, the arbitration clause may be drafted in any language and in any form or style.

9.3   Jurisdiction

The courts in the UAE will not hear an action if the parties have agreed to refer the matter to arbitration. However, this is not a matter of public policy and the person who is challenging the jurisdiction of the court must bring the fact that the parties have agreed to refer the matter to arbitration to the court's attention at the first hearing of the case.[3] The court will stay the proceedings and refer the parties to arbitration only if the jurisdiction of the court is challenged at the first hearing of the case. If not raised at the first hearing, the court will assume that the parties have waived their rights to refer the matter to arbitration and submit to the jurisdiction of the court. This is provided of course, that the arbitration clause is valid.

---

[1] Article 203(2) of the Civil Procedure Law.

[2] Supreme Court of Cassation Judgment 317 for the year 19 dated 29 November 1998, Supreme Court of Cassation Judgment 25 for the year 21 dated 9 January 2001, Dubai Court of Cassation Judgment 201/2001 dated 24 November 2001.

[3] Article 203(5) of the Law of Civil Procedure. Dubai Court of Cassation 235/99 dated 23 October 1999, Dubai Court of Cassation Judgment 138/2001 dated 9 June 2001.

In Dubai, the challenge must be brought at the first hearing of the case irrespective of whether the substantive submissions are also made by the defendant at that hearing. In Abu Dhabi and the Federal courts, challenging the jurisdiction must be brought the first time the defendant makes his submissions in response to the action, even if this is not actually the first hearing. The court in Abu Dhabi considers, for the purposes of Article 203(5) of the Civil Procedure Law, the making of the submission as the first hearing in which the defendant appears.

The court will normally hear the submissions and the arguments of the parties before reserving the case for judgment to determine whether to stay the court proceedings or not. On some occasions the court may decide to join such challenge to the merits of the case and request the parties to make their submissions on the jurisdiction of the court as well as on the merits of the case. The court will then decide on all the issues involved in the case, including arbitration, once the case has been reserved for judgment. In such circumstances, this will be a strong indication that the court has decided there is no valid arbitration clause. If however, the court decides to stay the proceedings, it will not look into the merits and the proceedings will be stayed on the grounds that the court has no jurisdiction.

9.4   Urgent and Interlocutory Applications

The fact that parties have agreed to refer a matter to arbitration does not prevent the courts from hearing urgent applications.

Arbitrators have limited powers when it comes to dealing with urgent and interlocutory applications as such measures do not constitute an award. It is established that even where an arbitration agreement exists, the power to grant such interim measures remains with the court. Thus, the court will hear applications such as the appointment of a custodian, a liquidator or for ordering an attachment against assets locally in the UAE. The court will always have jurisdiction to hear urgent applications or applications for an attachment against the assets irrespective of whether the parties have agreed to arbitration.[1] The only exception to this is if the parties have agreed in their agreement to refer all disputes, including any urgent applications or interlocutory applications that may be made by the parties in the future, to arbitration as well. While this is possible, the rules on this issue are unclear and there has been no precedent clarifying the issue.

---

[1] Dubai Court of Cassation Judgment 194/95 dated 9 March 1996, Dubai Court of Cassation Judgment 238/2000, 280/2000 and 291/2000 dated 26 November 2000, Dubai Court of Cassation Judgment 201/2001 dated 24 November 2001.

It is not clear how the parties would proceed with an attachment against assets in the UAE or file for an urgent application while the main action is being arbitrated locally or internationally. Amongst others, one of the issues which is of concern is the requirement under Article 255(2) of the Civil Procedure Law which requires the parties to bring the main action within 8 days after attachment.

The question that arises is whether bringing the arbitration proceedings within 8 days will satisfy the requirement under this Article or whether the party needs to bring an action before the court within 8 days, to uphold the attachment proceedings, in addition to the arbitration proceedings. The law is silent on this issue and there has been no clear indication from the court of the position. The principle in general, however, is that it is possible to obtain an attachment against an asset or to apply for an urgent application even if the parties have agreed to refer the matter to arbitration since urgent applications and orders for attachment fall outside the scope of the arbitrator unless the parties agree otherwise in their arbitration clause or during the arbitration process.

9.5 The Arbitration Tribunal

The parties to an agreement are free to appoint their own arbitrator and are also free to agree on the procedures for appointing an arbitrator to a tribunal. Normally, the two parties to arbitration will appoint their arbitrators and the arbitrators will choose the chairman of the tribunal. On other occasions the appointment will be left with a particular institute to appoint the arbitrator or tribunal according to the rules applicable to the process which they have agreed upon. This is all subject to the contents of the arbitration clause which the parties have agreed upon in their agreement or subsequently after notice of arbitration.

If either of the parties fail to proceed to arbitration or the parties have not agreed on the procedure or the name of the arbitrator, either party may apply to the court which essentially has jurisdiction to hear the dispute to enforce the arbitration clause and request the court to appoint the arbitrator[1] or to compel the other party to proceed with arbitration.

Such an application must be filed in the normal way before the court citing the relevant agreement and the arbitration clause and asking the court to either compel the other party to proceed to arbitration or to appoint an

---

[1] Article 204 of the Civil Procedure Law. Dubai Court of Cassation Judgment 271/96 dated 11 May 1997.

arbitrator. The court will normally hear the case in the normal course where both parties will be invited to make their submissions. The court will then make a decision whether to join the parties to arbitration and to appoint the arbitrator that has been agreed by the parties in the agreement or to appoint an arbitrator from the list registered with the court and request the parties to proceed with arbitration. Any order made by the court to proceed to arbitration will be subject to an appeal to the Court of Appeal and further to the Court of Cassation. The arbitration will not proceed until the judgment becomes final. The nomination of the arbitrator by the court is, however, not subject to appeal.[1]

If the parties have named an arbitrator in the agreement, the acceptance of the arbitrator must be in writing[2] and if he has not been named in the agreement the parties agreeing to a particular person to act as an arbitrator must also be in writing.

If arbitration is conducted by more that one arbitrator it must be an odd number[3] and decisions must be made by majority. All the arbitrators must hear the arguments, the submissions and sign the hearing record and the arbitration award.

Either party may object to the identity of an arbitrator. This is normally directed to the tribunal itself followed by a formal application to court to remove one or more of the arbitrators from the tribunal. Valid grounds must be set out before the court will entertain such an action, and normally only relates to serious issues such as doubts as to his impartiality or independence. Normally, such disclosure is expected immediately after the appointment of the arbitrator. Objection to an arbitrator must be made in the same manner and on the same grounds as an objection to a Judge in a court proceeding and within the prescribed time periods.[4]

9.5.1 Duties of an Arbitrator

An arbitrator who has been appointed in the proceedings must, within 30 days, inform the parties of the date of the first hearing to hear their arguments and submissions.[5] He must provide the parties with the date, the location and the time for the hearing. Proper service of summons must be

---

[1] Article 204(2) of the Civil Procedure Law.

[2] Article 207 of the Civil Procedure Law.

[3] Article 206(2) of the Civil Procedure Law.

[4] Article 207(4) of the Civil Procedure Law.

[5] Article 208 of the Civil Procedure Law.

effected on both parties to attend the hearing. The arbitrator may proceed with the arbitration in the absence of either party if a party fails to attend the arbitration proceeding or make a submission.

9.5.2 Powers of the Arbitrators

As is usual in a civil law system, there is only a limited discovery process. The arbitrators may order the parties to exhibit documents, call on witnesses, forward documents to be checked by the forensic laboratory (to ascertain whether they are forged if they are challenged by either of the parties during the arbitration process), appoint experts or take any action possible under the law. If such an order requires enforcement through the court or if one of the witnesses needs to be compelled to attend the arbitration or summons is to be served officially, the arbitrator (if the arbitration is conducted locally), may request the assistance of the court. The arbitrator will make an application to the Chief Justice of the court requesting the order to be enforced through the court. This is usually done by the arbitrator writing to the Chief Justice of the court providing him with information about the arbitration and the authority of the arbitrator which is derived from the arbitration agreement, the reasons why the assistance of the court is required and requesting the court to enforce the order.

An arbitrator has no power to impose a fine or to compel any party to do something or to request certain documents or information from a third party. Any action of this sort must be done through the court by a special application to the Chief Justice of the court who will decide on such application. The arbitrator may however, in his own discretion, decide to suspend the arbitration, if challenged by one of the parties or if an action has been filed before the court in other related matters or criminal proceedings which have been brought which may effect the decision made in the arbitration process. In such circumstances the arbitrator may also refer such a request or liaise with the Chief Justice of the court for guidelines.

Arbitrators need not follow the legal process which has been set out under the Civil Procedure Law designed for court actions. Arbitration will be conducted in accordance with the rules governing the arbitration or as agreed by the parties or as conducted by the arbitrator in the absence of rules.[1]

---

[1] Dubai Court of Cassation Judgment 260/94 and 261/94 dated 16 October 1994, Supreme Court of Cassation Judgment 433 for the year 17 dated 26 February 1997, Dubai Court of Cassation Judgment 173/96 dated 16 March 1997.

The following are exceptions to this:[1]

1. Parties may not settle the matter unless they are authorized to do so in the arbitration agreement.
2. There are certain issues which fall outside the jurisdiction of the arbitrators (such as criminal matters or a claim for forgery) and must be referred to the courts.
3. Arbitrators must approach the court for an order to compel a party to exhibit evidence needed for arbitration.
4. Arbitrators must approach the court for an order to compel a witness to appear before the tribunal.
5. Arbitrators must ask witnesses to take the prescribed oath before giving a statement.[2]

9.6 The Arbitration Award

The arbitration award will usually be delivered in majority and will be governed by the Civil Procedure Law relating to arbitration if delivered in the UAE[3]. If the arbitration award is delivered outside the UAE, it will be governed by the procedure that governs arbitration in the country where it has been delivered. An arbitration award must be accompanied by the arbitration agreement, contain a summary of the submissions made by the parties, the reasoning of the arbitrators and the date on which it was delivered and signed by all the arbitrators. If one of the arbitrators failed to sign the arbitration award, the arbitration award will be valid if it is signed by majority.[4]

The arbitration award usually needs to be delivered in Arabic,[5] however, the parties may agree for the arbitration award to be delivered in another language. If the arbitration award needs to be enforced in the UAE, it must be accompanied by an Arabic translation. An arbitration award is normally considered to be delivered on the date it has been signed.[6]

---

[1] Article 209 of the Civil Procedure Law.

[2] Article 211 of the Civil Procedure Law.

[3] Article 212(5) of the Civil Procedure Law.

[4] Article 212(5) of the Civil Procedure Law.

[5] Article 212(6) of the Civil Procedure Law.

[6] Article 212(7) of the Civil Procedure Law.

The arbitration award usually has to be delivered within 6 months from the first hearing[1] otherwise either party may pursue his case through the court in the normal way irrespective of the agreement to arbitrate. However, the parties may directly or by implication authorise the arbitrator to extend the period and the court, upon the request of the arbitrator, may also extend this period to an appropriate period.[2] It has been held by the UAE courts that continuing the arbitration after a period of 6 months where both parties continue to make submissions is considered an implied authorisation to the arbitrator to extend the period beyond 6 months.[3] Any objection to proceed with the case beyond 6 months must be brought to the attention of the arbitrator by the parties otherwise their silence is considered a consent to continue with the arbitration.

The arbitration tribunal's role in the arbitration will terminate once the final award has been issued. The tribunal has no role to play in the enforcement of the award. If, however, the arbitrators have been appointed by an order of court, they will have to file the arbitration award directly with the courts and may have to follow certain procedures under the particular rules which may be applicable, e.g. The Dubai Chamber of Commerce and Industry require a copy of the award to be filed with its Center for Commercial Conciliation and Arbitration.

9.7 Arbitration under the Supervision of the Court

If the arbitration was conducted under the supervision of the court, the action should be filed before the court. In such a case the matter will be referred to the arbitrator but the court will still have a general jurisdiction over the matter. In other words, if the arbitration is conducted independently of the court, the arbitration will proceed as normal without the interference of the court. However, if the parties ask the court to refer their dispute to arbitration and to uphold the clause, the court may refer the matter to arbitration and continue to supervise the arbitrators. The arbitrator will then be required to file the final arbitration award together with all supporting documents with the court for ratification within 15 days from the date on which the arbitration award was delivered.[4] A copy of it will be

---

[1] Article 210(1) of the Civil Procedure Law.

[2] Article 210(2) of the Civil Procedure Law.

[3] Dubai Court of Cassation Judgment 9/96 dated 13 July 1996, Supreme Court of Cassation Judgment 301 for the year 20 dated 13 December 1998.

[4] Article 213(1) of the Civil Procedure Law. Dubai Court of Cassation Judgment 31/2001 dated 11 March 2001.

delivered to both parties within 5 days from the date on which the arbitration award is lodged with the court. The Judge then will schedule a hearing within 15 days to ratify the arbitration award.

9.8 Enforcement of the Award

If the arbitration is conducted independently of the court, the arbitration award will be delivered by the arbitrator and copy of it will be delivered to the parties within 5 days from the date on which the arbitration award is delivered.

In the UAE, an award needs to be ratified by the courts for it to be equivalent to a court judgment and thereby enforceable against the losing party's assets. The UAE courts cannot consider the merits of the arbitrator's findings,[1] and an application to nullify an award will be purely on procedural grounds.

The parties must apply to the court independently for an order to ratify the arbitration award or to file a case to annul the arbitration award, as the case might be, depending on the parties who are filing the case. This will be by way of a normal Statement of Claim with supporting documents to be filed with the court in the normal course (after the payment of the fee). The court will then consider both party's arguments and submissions. The matter may involve several hearings where both parties will submit facts, evidence and arguments before the case is reserved for judgment. The court will decide whether to ratify or nullify the arbitration award.

A party may apply to the court to nullify the arbitration award at the time the court is looking into ratifying the arbitration award.[2] The court will consider whether to look into the application to nullify an arbitration award in the following circumstances:

Article 216 of the UAE Civil Procedure Law:

1. *If given without a deed of arbitration or if based on an invalid deed, or if lapsed through prescription, or if the arbitrators have exceeded the limits of the deed.*

---

[1] Article 217 of the Civil Procedure Law. Supreme Court of Cassation Judgment 165 for the year 18 dated 30 November 1996.

[2] Article 216 of the Civil Procedure Law. Supreme Court of Cassation Judgment 263 for the year 18 dated 8 December 1996.

2. *If the ruling has been given by arbitrators not appointed according to the law, or if given by some of them without being so empowered in the absence of the others, or if given under a deed of arbitration in which the subject of the dispute is not stated, or if given by someone not competent to agree to arbitration or by an arbitrator who does not fulfil the legal requirements.*
3. *If there is something invalid in the ruling or in the procedures affecting the ruling.*

It will not be possible for either party to waive their right to challenge the arbitration award if the grounds for annulment are based on one of the above. Parties are entitled to raise such a challenge even if they have waived their rights during the arbitration process.

In an application to ratify or to annul the arbitration award, the matter will follow the normal course of action before the court. The same procedures, applications, hearings and submissions will apply to the case and the period for appeal and other process will be identical to any other process as provided for in a normal action.

Therefore, in the UAE, in contrast to other jurisdictions, the ratification or nullification of the award becomes effectively the subject of a separate legal action and this is encouraged by defendants who wish to nullify an award on the basis of procedural errors. As mentioned, the claimant will not be able to enforce the arbitration award until it is converted into a final judgment confirming the validity of the original award. As a result, one of the purposes of arbitration (a speedy dispute resolution process) is defeated by what is time-wise, yet another trial between the same parties. Very rarely are arbitration awards issued within the 6-month time limit. Invariably there will be extensions agreed and granted. Thereafter the litigation process for authenticating the award could result in additional delays before final judgment is issued. The overall time consumed, may therefore be equal to or exceed the time spent before the courts in a straightforward litigation process.

9.9 Enforcement of a Foreign Arbitration Award

As mentioned, the UAE has not acceded to the New York Convention on the Recognition and Enforcement of Foreign Arbitral Awards and as such, at present, the principles which are applicable to the enforcement of foreign judgments pursuant to Article 236 of the Civil Procedure Law, will apply to the enforcement of foreign arbitration awards. However, the UAE Cabinet of Ministers have approved a suggestion made by the Minister of Justice to accede to the New York Convention and the matter has been put to the Supreme Council of the UAE for ratification.

The conditions set out under the Arab Convention on Judicial Cooperation (Riyadh) GCC Treaty or other co-operative arrangements or the bilateral agreements with France and India will apply to the enforcement of GCC state judgments or judgments delivered in France or India or vice-versa.[1] Accordingly, the conditions set out in the GCC Treaty or the bilateral agreements will supercede the conditions set out in Articles 235 to 238 of the Civil Procedure Law regarding the enforcement of foreign arbitration awards involving the GCC states, France or India and the UAE.[2]

In general, at present, in order to enforce a foreign arbitration award, an action must be brought before the UAE courts in the normal course requesting the court to ratify the foreign arbitration award and enforce the same locally. The court will only ratify the judgment after ascertaining that the following conditions, contained in Article 235 of the Civil Procedure Law have been satisfied:[3]

1. *That the State Courts do not have jurisdiction in the dispute in which the judgment has been given or the order made, and that the foreign Courts which issued it have jurisdiction therein under the international rules for legal jurisdiction prescribed in their laws.*
2. *That the judgment or order has been issued by a Court having jurisdiction under the law of the country in which issued.*
3. *That the opposing parties in the case in which the foreign judgment has been given have been summoned to appear, and have duly appeared.*
4. *That the judgment or order has acquired the force of a fait accompli under the law of the Court which issued it.*
5. *That it does not conflict with a judgment or order previously issued by a Court in the State and contains nothing in breach of public morals or order in the state.*

Each of these conditions are problematical and can be raised individually.

---

[1] See Appendix 2.

[2] Supreme Court of Cassation Judgment 41 for the year 17 dated 12 April 1998, Supreme Court of Cassation Judgment 236 for the year 19 dated 14 April 1998.

[3] Dubai Court of Cassation Judgment 17/2001 dated 10 March 2001.

In normal circumstances, when considering whether the judgment is good for execution, the court will apply the same standards and procedures that are applicable to the judgment in the country where the arbitration award was delivered. According to the UAE law[1] an arbitration award need not follow the UAE law of procedure and should only adhere to the procedure that is applicable in the country where the arbitration award has been delivered. However, on occasions the UAE courts go beyond this in an attempt to ensure that the judgment does not only satisfy the procedure in the country where it is delivered but also the UAE procedure.

Article 235(1) of the Civil Procedure Law reads as follows:

Judgments and orders issued in a foreign country may be executed in the UAE in the same conditions prescribed in the law of that country to execute the judgments and orders issued in the State.

Nevertheless, Judges in the UAE tend to ensure that the arbitration award satisfies the UAE law of procedure as well as the foreign procedure and this practice seems to exceed the meaning of the Article.

It is quite difficult to enforce a foreign arbitration award in the UAE, especially if it is based on foreign rules. The court tends to request evidence that the arbitration award is final and good for execution in the country where the arbitration award was delivered.[2] In other words, the courts in the UAE are not satisfied with the fact that the arbitration award is valid and delivered according to the process in the country where it is delivered according to the laws and regulations in that country and the agreement of the parties, but also need evidence that the arbitration award is final and good for execution before the court of that country. Such evidence must be of strong judicial authority and an affidavit or advice from legal counsel will not satisfy such a requirement.

The UAE courts also try to ensure that the party was properly summoned to attend the hearing and that service was properly effected on them, especially in the case where the arbitration award was given in default.

Whilst bilateral agreements are recognized by the UAE courts, in the absence of such agreement evidence must be provided that the two countries have a mutual enforceability of foreign awards policy. This is

---

[1] Article 235(1) of the Civil Procedure Law.

[2] Dubai Court of Cassation Judgment 267/99 dated 27 November 1999, Dubai Court of Cassation Judgment 17/2001 dated 10 March 2001.

often difficult to prove in the absence of precedent, specific agreement or specific provisions in the country's law.

Once the arbitration award is ratified, whether it is local or international, it will be good for execution once it becomes final. Execution of the arbitration award will go through the same process as that of execution of a judgment according to the Civil Procedure Law for the execution of judgments through the court Execution Department. The final order ratifying the foreign arbitration award will be considered equal to a judgment delivered by the UAE court.

In Dubai, it is not possible for the Dubai Government or any of the Dubai Government's departments, agencies or authorities to enter into any agreement for foreign arbitration unless a special consent is given by the Government authorising the department, agency or authority to enter into such an arbitration agreement.[1]

When looking into ratifying the arbitration award, the court will not look into the merits of the case, the facts or the evidence and will only ensure that the arbitration award has complied with the formalities required under the law and that both the parties have been afforded the right to defend themselves and to present their case properly according to the principles of justice and fair trial.[2]

Once the UAE accedes to the New York Convention, however, the conditions set out in the New York Convention will be applicable to the enforcement of foreign arbitration awards in the UAE. This is a very welcome development and will have a major impact on the enforcement of foreign arbitration awards in the UAE.

9.10 Appeal

While the arbitration award itself is not subject to any appeal, the judgment delivered by the court to ratify or nullify the arbitration award is subject to an appeal to the Court of Appeal and further to the Court of Cassation.[3] It is

---

[1] Article 36 of Dubai Law No. 6 of 1997 concerning Contracts of Government Departments in the Emirate of Dubai.

[2] Supreme Court of Cassation Judgment 371 for the year 18 dated 30 June 1998, Supreme Court of cassation Judgment 157 for the year 19 dated 25 April 1999.

[3] Dubai Court of Cassation Judgment 186/96 dated 5 January 1997.

procedurally impossible for the arbitration award to be executed before final judgment is delivered.

On occasions the Judges are empowered to refer the matter back to the arbitrator to deal with issues that they have failed to deal with or to deal with aspects of the arbitration award which they may have failed to clarify. In such a case the arbitrator must provide his final decision on the matter within 3 months from the date on which the arbitration award was returned to him to be amended or supplemented.[1] The decision from the court to refer the matter back to arbitration is not subject to an appeal until final judgment is delivered on the application to ratify the award or to nullify the award. It cannot be appealed independently from this application.

9.11 Costs

The arbitrators themselves determine the costs in an arbitration award. Arbitrators normally will award the costs to the claimant or may even split the costs between the two parties depending on the outcome of the arbitration. However, on occasions when the costs (other than the subject matter of the arbitration) awarded by the arbitrator is quite high or the interest is excessive, the court may interfere in the arbitration award and reduce the award or the interest rate awarded in connection therewith. However, such power will only be exercised in limited and unusual circumstances.

Both the Dubai and the Abu Dhabi Chambers of Commerce Centres for Conciliation and Arbitration have a schedule of costs which the arbitrator must follow, unless agreed otherwise. If the arbitrator is a court appointed arbitrator, the court may order the party to deposit into court, a deposit to cover the costs of the arbitration to be assessed by the court when the final award is filed. The arbitrator in such a case will have to apply to court to release payment, unless agreed otherwise by the parties. The costs of the arbitration will include any other costs associated with the arbitration, such as experts fees, witness costs or otherwise.

---

[1] Article 214 of the Civil Procedure Law. Dubai Court of Cassation Judgment 17/2001 dated 10 March 2001.

Appendix 1

Court Fee Structure

Courts	Abu Dhabi	Dubai
First Instance	4% for claim less than AED 5,000 Max. AED 10,000 5% for claim more than AED 5,000 Min. AED 50	7.5% for the first and second AED 100,000 6% for the third AED 100,000 5% for any claim exceeding AED 300,000 Max. AED 30,000 Min. AED 10
Appeal	4% for claim less than AED 5,000 Max. AED 10,000 5% for claim more than AED 5,000 Min. AED 50	1.5% for the first and second AED 100,000 1.2% for the third AED 100,000 1% for any amount over AED 300,000 Max. AED 6,000
Cassation	AED 500 + (AED 1,000 as deposit to be refunded)	AED 500 + (AED 1,000 as deposit to be refunded)
Attachment	4% for claim less than AED 5,000 5% for claim more than AED 5,000 Max. AED 10,000 Min. AED 50 Claim and Attachment may be filed together with one fee for both. If attachment filed prior to action then fees to be paid for the main claim in addition.	50% from the First Instance fee Max. AED 15,000
Execution	AED 100 as advance and 1/3 of the 1st Instance fee paid Min. AED 50	1% Max. AED 5,000 Min. AED 10

Courts	Sharjah	Al Ain
First Instance	4% for claim less than AED 5,000 Max. AED 10,000 5% for claim more than AED 5,000 Min. AED 50	4% for claim less than AED 5,000 Max. AED 10,000 5% for claim more than AED 5,000 Min. AED 50
Appeal	4% for claim less than AED 5,000 Max. AED 10,000 5% for claim more than AED 5,000 Min. AED 50 (Amount appealed + Fee of 1st Instance + Adv. Fee + Interest on the adjudged amount until the date of filing the appeal)	4% for claim less than AED 5,000 Max. AED 10,000 5% for claim more than AED 5,000 Min. AED 50
Cassation	In Abu Dhabi High Court	In Abu Dhabi High Court
Attachment	4% for claim less than AED 5,000 5% for claim more than AED 5,000 Max. AED 10,000 Min. AED 50 Claim and Attachment may be filed together with one fee for both. If attachment filed prior to action then fees to be paid for the main claim in addition.	4% for claim less than AED 5,000 5% for claim more than AED 5,000 Max. AED 10,000 Min. AED 50 Claim and Attachment may be filed together with one fee for both. If attachment filed prior to action then fees to be paid for the main claim in addition.
Execution	AED 100 as advance and 1/3 of the 1st Instance fee paid Min. AED 50	AED 100 as advance and 1/3 of the 1st Instance fee paid Min. AED 50

Courts	Ajman	Umm Al Quwain
First Instance	4% for claim less than AED 5,000 Max. AED 10,000 5% for claim more than AED 5,000 Min. AED 50	4% for claim less than AED 5,000 Max. AED 10,000 5% for claim more than AED 5,000 Min. AED 50
Appeal	4% for claim less than AED 5,000 Max. AED 10,000 5% for claim more than AED 5,000 Min. AED 50 (Amount appealed + Fee of 1st Instance + Adv. Fee + Interest of the judged amount till the date of filing the appeal)	4% for claim less than AED 5,000 Max. AED 10,000 5% for claim more than AED 5,000 Min. AED 50 (Amount appealed + Fee of 1st Instance + Adv. Fee + Interest of the judged amount till the date of filing the appeal)
Cassation	In Abu Dhabi High Court	In Abu Dhabi High Court
Attachment	4% for claim less than AED 5,000 5% for claim more than AED 5,000 Max. AED 10,000 Min. AED 50 Claim and Attachment may be filed together with one fee for both. If attachment filed prior to action then fees to be paid for the main claim in addition.	4% for claim less than AED 5,000 5% for claim more than AED 5,000 Max. AED 10,000 Min. AED 50 Claim and Attachment may be filed together with one fee for both. If attachment filed prior to action then fees to be paid for the main claim in addition.
Execution	AED 100 as advance and 1/3 of the 1st Instance fee paid Min. AED 50	AED 100 as advance and 1/3 of the 1st Instance fee paid Min. AED 50

Courts	Fujairah	Khorfakkan	Ras Al Khaimah
First Instance	4% for claim less than AED 5,000 Max. AED 10,000 5% for claim more than AED 5,000 Min. AED 50	4% for claim less than AED 5,000 Max. AED 10,000 5% for claim more than AED 5,000 Min. AED 50	10% Max AED 30,000 AED 10,000 if unlimited amount
Appeal	4% for claim less than AED 5,000 Max. AED 10,000 5% for claim more than AED 5,000 Min. AED 50 (Amount appealed + Fee of 1st Instance + Adv. Fee + Interest of the adjudged amount until the date of filing the appeal)	Appeal should be filed in the Court of Fujairah.	5% Max AED 15,000
Cassation	In Abu Dhabi High Court	In Abu Dhabi High Court	No Cassation Court
Attachment	4% for claim less than AED 5,000 5% for claim more than AED 5,000 Max. AED 10,000 Min. AED 50 Claim and Attachment may be filed together with one fee for both. If attachment filed prior to action then fees to be paid for the main claim in addition.	4% for claim less than AED 5,000 5% for claim more than AED 5,000 Max. AED 10,000 Min. AED 50 Claim and Attachment may be filed together with one fee for both. If attachment filed prior to action then fees to be paid for the main claim in addition.	10% Max. AED 3000 If the main action was filed, no fee
Execution	AED 100 as advance and 1/3 of the 1st Instance fee paid Min. AED 50	AED 100 as advance and 1/3 of the 1st Instance fee paid Min. AED 50	1% Max. AED 5,000 Min. AED 10

Appendix 2

Agreements on Judicial Cooperation & the Enforcement of Judgments to which the UAE has Acceded or has Signed

Country	Agreement	Decree No.	Date	Remarks
International (New York)	New York Convention on the Recognition and Enforcement of Foreign Arbitral Awards (1958)			UAE has not formally acceded although approved by the Cabinet of Ministers and awaiting Decision of Supreme Council of UAE.
International (Geneva)	European Convention on International Commercial Arbitration			UAE has not acceded
Tunisia	Agreement on Judicial Cooperation, Enforcement of Judgments & Extradition of Criminals	32/ 1975	15.05.75	Deals with the enforcement of arbitral awards in Article 23 and the enforcement of judgments in civil and commercial matters and personal status matters and judgments rendered in civil matters heard by criminal courts.

#	Country	Agreement	Decree No.	Date	Remarks
4.	Morocco	Agreement on Judicial Cooperation, Service of Process, Letters Rogatory and Extradition of Criminals	80/ 1978	18.12.78	Deals with the enforcement of arbitral awards in Article 21 and the enforcement of judgments in civil and commercial matters and personal status matters and judgments rendered in civil matters heard by criminal courts.
5.	Syria	Agreement on Legal & Judicial Cooperation in Civil, Commercial, Personal Status and Criminal Matters	12/ 1980	20.01.80	Deals with the enforcement of arbitral awards in Article 29 and the enforcement of judgments in civil and commercial matters and personal status matters and judgments rendered in civil matters heard by criminal courts.
6.	Somalia	Agreement on Legal & Judicial Cooperation	95/ 1982	17.12.82	Deals with the enforcement of arbitral awards in Article 29 and the enforcement of judgments in civil and commercial matters and personal status matters and judgments rendered in civil matters heard by criminal courts.

Country	Agreement	Decree No.	Date	Remarks
Algeria	Agreement on Judicial Cooperation, Service of Process, Letters Rogatory, Enforcement of Judgments and Extradition of Criminals			Deals with the enforcement of arbitral awards in Article 21 and the enforcement of judgments in civil and commercial matters and personal status matters and judgments rendered in civil matters heard by criminal courts.
France	Convention on Judicial Cooperation and the Recognition & Enforcement of Judgments in Civil & Commercial Matters	31/ 1992	27.04.92	Deals with the enforcement of arbitral awards in Article 17 and the reciprocal enforcement of judgments.
GCC	Agreement on the Enforcement of Judgments, Letters Rogatory and Service of Process	41/ 1996	17.06.96	Does not include the enforcement of arbitral awards. Deals with the enforcement of judgments in civil, commercial, administrative and personal status matters.

#	Country	Agreement	Decree No.	Date	Remarks
10.	The Riyadh Convention	The Arab Convention on Judicial Cooperation (Riyadh)	53/ 1999	15.04.99	Deals with the enforcement of arbitral awards in Article 27 and the enforcement of judgments in civil, commercial, administrative and personal status matters Signatories to the Convention: 1- Jordan, 2- UAE, 3- Bahrain, 4- Tunisia, 5- Algeria, 6- Djibouti, 7- Saudi Arabia, 8- Sudan, 9- Syria, 10- Somalia, 11- Iraq, 12- Oman, 13- Palestine, 14- Qatar, 15- Kuwait, 16- Lebanon, 17- Libya & 18- Morocco.
11.	Jordan	Agreement on Legal & Judicial Cooperation	106/ 1999	24.11.99	Deals with the enforcement of arbitral awards in Article 25 and the reciprocal enforcement of final judgments

#	Country	Agreement	Decree No.	Date	Remarks
12.	India	Agreement on Legal and Judicial Cooperation in Civil and Commercial Matters, Mutual Legal Assistance in Criminal Matters & Extradition of Criminals	33/ 2000	31.03.00	Deals with the enforcement of arbitral awards in Article 25 and the enforcement of judgments in civil and commercial matters and personal status matters and judgments rendered in civil matters heard by criminal courts.
13.	Egypt	Agreement on Legal & Judicial Assistance.	83/ 2000	10.07.00	Deals with the enforcement of arbitral awards in Article 38 and the enforcement of judgments in civil and commercial matters and personal status matters and judgments rendered in civil matters heard by criminal courts
14.	Syria	Agreement on Legal & Judicial Cooperation in Civil and Commercial Matters, Criminal Matters and Personal Status Matters with Extradition and Assistance in the Settlement of Estate	60/ 2002	13.11.02	Deals with the enforcement of arbitral awards in Article 41 and the enforcement of judgments in civil and commercial matters, personal status matters and judgments rendered in matters related to recovery of damages and property heard by criminal courts.

INDEX

Abu Dhabi
　arbitration center, 147
　Shari'a Court, 14-5
　substantive matters, 2
Adjournment
　auction, 103, 109
　case, 11, 53, 63, 130, 138
Administrative disputes
　Federal Government, 26-7
　local government, 27
Admission
　lawyer, as a, 6-7
　of liability, 71
Advocates, 6, 43, 134
Agreements, reciprocal, 30, 33-9, 148, 158, 167-71
Alimony, 20, 115, 120
Anton Pillar orders, 5
Appeal
　arbitration awards, ratification of, 161
　attachment, against, 83-4, 125
　automatic right to, 11, 16, 125
　counter-appeal, 127-28, 131-32
　criminal cases, 13-4
　default judgment, 68-9
　execution procedural matters, 134
　formalities, 135
　grounds of, 11-2, 126
　hearing, 138
　interim judgment, 70
　leave of the Court, 11-2
　notification, 127, 137
　precautionary matter, 70, 125
　preferent claims, 117
　remedies, additional, 128
　second appeal, 142-43

　sub-appeal, 131-32
Arbitration
　agreement, 24, 37, 149-50, 154, 160
　attachment, 150-51
　Civil Procedure Law, 149, 153-54, 158
　clauses, 149, 151
　costs, 147-48, 161
　Dubai Government, 160
　evidence, 149, 153-54
　experts, 153
　fair trial, 160
　foreign law, 30
　interim measures, 150
　law, 147-49, 159
　procedural rules, 147, 149
　subject of, 148
　time-limits, 151-52, 155-56
Arbitration awards
　appeal, 128, 142, 160-61
　execution of, 159-60
　foreign awards, 23, 31, 37-8, 148, 157-60
　international arbitration agreements, 148, 158, 167-71
　New York Convention, 148, 157, 160, 167
　nullification of, 156-57, 160
　ratification of, 156-58, 160
　UAE law of procedure, 159
Arbitration centers, 147-48, 161
Arbitrators
　acceptance, 152
　appointment, 149, 151, 156
　appointed by the Court, 151-52, 155
　assistance of the Court, 153-54

objection to, 152
supervision of, 155
Arrangements, co-operative, 30, 33, 148, 158, 167-71
Attachment
  challenging application, 89-90
  conditions for enforcement, 85-6
  counterfeit goods, 85
  experts, 87
  extreme urgency, 77, 86
  insolvency of defendant, 91
  movable property, 23, 107
  non-attachable assets, 74
  order *ex parte*, 73, 76, 79
  precautionary-, 70, 73, 105, 114, 125
  real estate property, 90
  ships, 75-6, 85, 107
  supervision by claimant, 77
  suspension of, 88, 90
  third party claim to ownership, 89
  see also Arbitration
Attendance in Court, 67, 69
Attorney appointed by Court, 13
Attorney General, 27

Bad faith, 91
Bail, 13, 122
Bank guarantee, 139-40
Bankruptcy, 17, 20
Bar Association, 7-8

Chamber of Commerce, 147, 161
Chief Justice of the Court, 44, 77, 86, 94, 153
Civil matters,
  amicable settlement, 41-3
  claims, 11
  Federal Law, 9
  minors, 65

right of appeal, 11-2
Shari'a Courts, 15
submissions, 11-2
victim of crime, 13
see also Minors; Submissions
Civil Procedure Law, 9, 19, 24, 26, 41, 47, 71, 73, 149, 153-54, 158
Clerk of the Court
  appeal, 126-27, 137-38
  enforcement of attachment, 85-6
  Statement of Claim, 43-4, 76
  summons, 45
  translator, 57
Commercial instruments, 71-2
Commercial matters
  arbitration, 147
  books of account, 63
  debts, 71-2
  jurisdiction, 21
Common law, 5
Companies
  custodian, 95
  employee, 50, 116
  head office, 21-2, 46
  liquidation, 70, 130
Conciliation, 147
Confidentiality, 57, 123
Confiscation, 118
Conflicting evidence, 56
Conflict of interest, 46
Conflict of laws, 4, 30
Constitutional matters, 16
Construction industry, 5, 92
Contempt of Court, 129
Contracts
  common law, 5
  governing law, 29-30
  jurisdiction, 20
Convictions, 57
Costs

arbitration, 147-48, 161
auction, 111
custodian, 96
translations, 17-8
Counterclaims
requirements, 54
subject matter, 54-5
timing, 54-5
Court bailiff, 45, 50, 68, 77, 86, 88-9, 106-07, 109, 118
Court of Appeal, 4, 11, 65, 83, 101, 125-29, 132-34, 141-42, 152, 160
Court of Cassation *see* Dubai; Supreme Court of Cassation
Court of First Instance, 65, 80, 85, 129, 132-33, 144
Criminal actions
civil claim, 13, 122
electronic signatures, 61
Federal Law, 9
Prosecutor's Office, 12-3, 122
release on bail, 13, 122
right to appeal, 13
Shari'a Courts, 14-5
submissions, 13
types of crimes, 12
victim, 13
Custodian, 70, 86-8, 92, 94-6, 111, 116, 150

Debt
concurrent-, 114
government-, 115
installment plan, 120
maritime-, 116
port charges, 107, 115
preferent-, 114, 117
recoveries, 15, 71
rent, 116
settlement, 119
wages, 116

Decree, 1, 9, 23
Default by defendant, 68
Defendants
counterclaim, 53-5
joinder of, 63-4
summary judgment, 71-2
Delay
arbitration, 157
auction, 113
Delaying tactics, 60, 102
Deputation, 47, 94
Discovery, 5, 62, 153
Dispensation, 44
Dispute Resolution Office *see* Labour disputes
Disputes between Emirates, 16
Documents
authentication, 9-10
deputation, 94
discovery, 5
electronic messages, 62
fax copies, 61
forged-, 143-44, 153
notarisation, 10
Domicile, 19-22, 36, 69
Dubai
arbitration center, 147, 155
Court fees, 10, 163
Court of Cassation, 4, 11, 12, 16, 82, 134
judicial system, 4
licence to practice, 7
prosecutor's office, 4
Rents Committee, 25-6
substantive matters, 2

Education and training, 6-7
Egypt
legal education, 6
legal system, 5
Employees *see* Companies; Labour disputes

Enforcement of judgments
   challenging the proceedings, 102
   suspension of, 138
   see also Foreign judgments

Evidence
   arbitration, 149, 154
   cassation, 15
   contradictory-, 56
   expert witnesses see Experts
   foreign judgments, 32
   foreign law provisions, 30
   merchant's books, 63
   notarisation of documents, 10
   urgent proceedings, 93

Execution of judgment
   appeal, 101, 117-18, 130, 134, 142
   auction procedure, 102-14
   challenge proceedings, 100-02, 117-18
   confinement of debtor, 120-21
   Execution Department, 85-6, 97-8, 108, 114, 118, 122
   fees, 99, 116
   final payment, 119-20
   foreign judgment, 32, 34-5
   notice, 99, 109
   supervision by creditor, 114, 118
   suspension of, 16, 101-02, 119, 138-40

Experts
   appointed by the Court, 87, 105-06, 110
   criminal cases, 13
   definition, 58
   fees, 18, 59
   immovable property, 109
   mandate, 58-9
   report, 59
   selection procedure, 58

   urgent proceedings, 92

Fair trial, principle of, 160
False statements, 144
Family matters, 14, 17, 30, 34, 42, 143
Federal Courts, 4, 9-18
Federal Government
   administrative actions, 26-7
   jurisdiction, 2, 4
   Ministry of Justice, 4, 6-7, 9-10, 48, 58
Federal Judicial Authority, 4, 41
Federal laws, 2, 4
Fees
   advocates, 116
   Court, 10, 17, 44, 54, 72, 76, 99, 116, 136, 163-66
   exemption of, 17, 44
   expert, 18, 128, 161
   joinder, 64
   notarisation, 10
   rent committee, 26
Force majeur clause, 5
Foreign law, 30
Foreign judgments
   conditions for enforcement, 31
   ratification, 32, 34
   reciprocal treaties, 33-9, 167-71
   requirements, 32
Foreign proceedings, 24
Forgery, 56, 60, 154
Forum non-convenience principle, 29
France, 36-7, 148, 169
Fraud, 144
Free zone areas
   jurisdiction, 27-8

GCC Treaty, 30, 33-6, 148, 158, 169
Guardianship *see* Minors

Hearings
   arbitration, 150, 152, 155
   Court of Cassation, 15, 138
   urgent application, 93
   withdrawal from, 69

Impartiality, 152
Indemnity, 64
India, 38, 148, 171
Inheritance, 20, 22, 143
Insolvency, 22, 91, 121
Insurance policy claims, 22
Interlocutory judgment *see* Judgments
International agreements, 30, 33-39, 148, 158, 167-71
Islamic Law *see* Shari'a

Joinder of actions, 13, 55, 127
Joinder of parties, 63-5
Judges, 6, 9
Judgments
   default-, 68-9
   ex parte, 71-2, 125
   foreign *see* Foreign judgments
   in absentia, 67
   interim-, 70-1
   interlocutory-, 125
   on procedure, 125
   service of, 68-9
   summary-, 71-2
   suspension of, 139
Judicial review, 15, 37-8, 143-45
Judicial system, 4-5
Judiciaries, 9-10
Jurisdiction
   appeal, 129, 133, 142
   arbitration, 149-50, 155
   domestic, 21-22
   emirates, 4, 21, 28
   Federal Government, 2, 4
   interim judgment, 70

   international, 19-21
   objections, 125
   Shari'a Courts, 14
Jurist Association, 7-8
Justice
   in the interests of, 65
   principles of, 160

Labour disputes
   appeal, 142
   claims, 116
   Dispute Resolution Office, 25
   employee remuneration, 22, 116
Lands Department, 23, 100, 109
Law firms, 5, 7
Law of Civil Procedure *see* Civil Procedure Law
Lawyers
   confidentiality, 57
   fees, 116
   licence to practice, 6-7, 134-35
Leave of the Court
   joinder of actions, 13
   right of appeal, 11
Legal aid, 13
Legal principles, 15-6
Lex situs, 29
Liability, 36, 64, 71
Local affairs, 1
Local Courts, 4, 10-11
Local laws, 4, 30

Mareva injunction, 5
Maritime Code, 24
Maritime disputes
   arrest of vessel, 23, 107
   attachment, 75-6, 85, 107
   urgent proceedings, 92
Mediation
   labour disputes, 25
Ministry of Justice *see* Federal Government

Ministry of labour and Social Affairs, 25
Minors
   actions by and against, 65
   debtor, 121
   guardianship, 14, 20
   Prosecutor's Office, 65
Misleading the Court, 143
Mortgage, 107, 111, 113, 116, 118

New York Convention, 148, 157, 167
Notaries, 9-10
Notification
   appeal, 127, 137-38
   attachment order, 73, 76
   execution proceedings, 99, 109-10
   judgment *ex parte*, 72

Oral arguments, 5, 11

Petition, 34, 47, 68, 108
Police force, 4, 122
Power of Attorney, 43, 136
Precautionary matters, 70, 73, 125
Precedents, 5, 15
Preferent claims, 114-18
Preliminary arguments, 53-4
Prescription, 42, 119
Pre-trial motions, 53
Property claims
   granted land, 23
   immovable-, 19, 23, 29, 90-1, 103, 109-14, 138-40
   movable-, 23-4, 104-08
Prosecutor's office, 4, 12-3, 65, 122
Public auction *see* Execution of judgments
Public international law, 37
Public policy, 10, 19, 21, 34, 57, 149

Ras Al Khaimah
   court fees, 10
   judicial system, 4
   licence to practice, 7
   Shari'a Court, 14-5
Real estate property *see* Property claims
Reconciliation Committee
   agreement, 43
   application, 42
   committees, 41-3
Remedies
   attachment, 78, 79, 81
   confiscation, 118
   documents, to file, 64
Renewal of case, 69-70
Rent disputes
   Complaints Committee, 26
   jurisdiction, 22
   Rent Committee, 25-6, 42
Restraining orders, 74
Review application, 144
Ruler, 1-3, 9, 17, 23, 27

Service of summons
   agent, on, 45
   announcement, by, 50
   employee, on, 50
   improper-, 52
   legal entity, on, 46
   political channels, via, 48
   proof of, 48
   publication, by, 49-50
   responsibility claimant, 46, 49
Settlement
   agreement, 119
   amicable-, 41-3
Shari'a,
   Courts, 14-5
   Islamic Law, 5, 35

    Islamic schools of, 14
    principles, 34
    research, 8
Sharjah
    Complaints Committee, 26
Ships *see* Maritime Disputes
Sources of law, 5, 8
Statement of Claim, 43-5, 75, 79, 128, 156
Stay of proceedings, 53, 149-50
Submissions
    Civil Court, 11, 53
    Court of Appeal, 11, 126
    Court of Cassation, 11, 15, 138
    Criminal Court, 12
Supreme Court of Cassation, 4, 12, 14-6, 101, 129, 131-32, 134-43, 152, 160

Third party
    challenge, 89-90, 104
    claims, 107, 113
    covering for damages, 85
    objection, 111
    reclaiming assets, 104
Time limits
    appeal, 11, 14, 68-9, 125, 131, 134-35, 138
    attachment order *ex parte*, 76, 79
    defendant's response, 52-3
    Reconciliation Committees, 42
    objection to judgment, 72
    summons, 45

Tort, 5
Trademark claims, 75, 85, 118
Translations, 17-8, 57, 154

Union Declaration, 1
University Law School, 6
Urgent matters
    appointment of custodian, 94-6
    appointment of surveyor, 92
    arbitration, 150-51
    attachment, 70, 76, 83
    hearing of witness *see*
Witnesses

Valuation, 105-06, 110

Wages, 116
Waiving of rights, 57, 149, 157
Witnesses
    arbitration, 153
    attachment cases, 83
    challenge of, 57
    counter, 56
    criminal cases, 13
    deputation to hear, 94
    expert- *see* Experts
    false testimony, 144
    number of, 57
    urgent application to hear, 93

ARAB AND ISLAMIC LAWS SERIES

1. *Islamic Law and Finance,* Chibli Mallat (ed.) (1988)
(ISBN 1-85333-121-X)

2. *The Islamic Laws of Personal Status* (2nded.), Jamal 1. Nasir (1990)
(ISBN 1-85333-280-1)

3. *Islamic Family Law,* Chibli Mallat and Jane Connors (eds.) (1991)
(ISBN 1-85333-301-8)

4. *Mixed Courts of Egypt,* Mark S.W. Hoyle (1991)
(ISBN 1-85333-321-2)

5. *The Theory of Contracts in Islamic Law,* S.E. Rayner (1991)
(ISBN 1-85333-617-3)

6. *The Marriage Contract in Islamic Law,* Dawoud S. El Alami (1992)
(ISBN 1-85333-719-6)

7. *Unlawful Gain and Legitimate Profit in Islamic Law,* Nabil A. Saleh (1992)
(ISBN 1-85333-721-8)

8. *Islamic and Public Law,* Chibli Mallat (ed.) (1993)
(ISBN 1-85333-768-4)

9. *Finance of International Trade in the Gulf,* Dr. Ahmed A.M.S. Al-Suwaidi (1994)
(ISBN 1-85333-947-4)

10. *The Law of Commercial Procedure of the United Arab Emirates,* Dawoud S., El Alami (1994)
(ISBN 1-85966-080-0)

11. *The Status of Women under Islamic Law* (2nd ed.), Jamal J. Nasir (1995)
(ISBN 1-85966-084-3)

12. *Business Laws of Yemen,* Abdulla M.A. Maktari and John McHugo (1995)
(ISBN 1-85966-112-2)

13. *Arab Islamic Banking and Renewal of Islamic Law,* Nicholas D. Ray (1995)
(ISBN 1-85966-104-1)

14. *The Law of Business Contracts in the Arab Middle East,* Nayla Cornair-Obeid (1996)
(ISBN 90-411-0216-7)

KLUWER LAW INTERNATIONAL – THE HAGUE, LONDON, NEW YORK

ARAB AND ISLAMIC LAWS SERIES

15. *Islamic Institutions in Jerusalem,* Yitzhak Reiter (1997)
(ISBN 90-411-0382-1)

16. *Islamic Law and Finance: Religion, Risk and Return,* Frank E. Vogel and Samuel L. Hayes III (1998)
(ISBN 90-411-0547-6)

17. *United Arab Emirates Court of Cassation Judgments* 1989-1997, Richard Price and Essam Al Tamimi (1998)
(ISBN 90-411-1005-4)

18. *Legal Pluralism in the Arab World,* Baudouin Dupret, Maurits Berger, and Laila al-Zwaini (eds.) (1999)
(ISBN 90-411-1005-0)

19. *Intellectual Property Laws of the Arab Countries,* Abu-Ghazaleh (2000)
(ISBN 90-411-8842-8)

20. *An Introduction to Islamic Finance,* Mohammad Taqi Usmani (2001)
(ISBN 90-411-1619-2)

21. *Studies in Modern Islamic Law and Jurisprudence,* O. Arabi (2001)
(ISBN 90-411-1660-5)

22. *Egypt and its Laws,* G. Alleaume, N. Bernard-Maugiron and B. Dupret (eds.) (2001)
(ISBN 90-411-1639-7)

23. *The Islamic Law of Personal Status, Third Edition,* Jamal J. Nasir (2001)
(ISBN hb: 90-411-1661-3; pb: 90-411-1663-X)

24. *Arbitral Awards of the Cairo Regional Centre for International Commerical Arbitration II*, M.E.I. Alam Eldin (2003)
(ISBN 90-411-1946-9)

25. *Judiciary and Arbitration in Bahrain,* H.A. Radhi (2003)
(ISBN 90-411-2217-6)

26. *Practical Guide to Litigation and Arbitration in the United Arab Emirates,* Essam Al Tamimi (2003)
(ISBN 90-411-2221-4)

KLUWER LAW INTERNATIONAL – THE HAGUE, LONDON, NEW YORK